Dr. Laura:
A Mother in America

Dr. Laura:
A Mother in America

Christian Insights about
America's Best-Known Mom

by
Minister Ray McClendon

Chariot Victor Publishing
A Division of Cook Communications

Chariot Victor Publishing
Cook Communications, Colorado Springs, Colorado 80918
Cook Communications, Paris, Ontario
Kingsway Communications, Eastbourne, England

DR. LAURA: A MOTHER IN AMERICA

Cover Design: Bill Gray
Interior Design: Pat Miller
Cover Photo: Sylvia Mautner

Unless otherwise noted, all Scripture references are taken from the *Holy Bible, New International Version®*. Copyright © 1973, 1978, 1984 by International Bible Society. Used by permision of Zondervan Publishing House. All rights reserved. Other references are taken from *The New King James Version* (NKJV), © 1979, 1980, 1982, Thomas Nelson, Inc., Publishers; the *Jerusalem Bible* (JB), published and copyrighted 1966, 1967, and 1968 by Darton, Longman & Todd Ltd. and Doubleday & Co., Inc. and used by permission of the publisher; and the *King James Version* (KJV).

1 2 3 4 5 6 7 8 9 10 Printing/Year 03 02 01 00 99

Library of Congress Cataloging-in-Publication Data

McClendon, Ray.
    Dr. Laura: a mother in America/by Ray McClendon.
      p. cm.
    ISBN 1564767728
    1. Interpersonal relations—Religious aspects—Christianity.
    2. Interpersonal relations—Biblical teaching. 3. Schlessinger, Laura. I.
Title. II. Title: Doctor Laura.
BV4597.52.M398   1999   99-17557
248—dc21 CIP

Dedication

For my wife, Linda . . .

Who, like God, has been
more patient and loving with me
than I deserve.

. . . and our children.
May the seeds of faith we've planted
in their hearts flourish and blossom.

Table of Contents

Acknowledgments

You learn a lot about yourself writing a first book. Some of it I'd just as soon not know (wry smile). But, like so much else in life, our more difficult challenges are those from which we derive the most benefit.

I'm very grateful to Dr. Laura Schlessinger for suggesting this book idea in the first place, then making her office and program materials so freely available to me. Her permission to use entire calls and monologues, which I then used to frame my comments and biblical references, was very gracious. She has read a lot of my "stuff" on the air and commented on it. Now I get to cite her "stuff" and comment on it. We do make a pretty good team now and then. In that sense, it can be fairly said that we coauthored this book. It is hers as much as it is mine, which is one of the main reasons I am donating a portion of all royalties to the Dr. Laura Schlessinger Foundation.

My sincere thanks also to her marvelous staff, who made me feel right at home and went out of their way to assist me. Keven Bellows (thanks for thinking of those transcripts!), Amir Henrickson, "Cousin Carolyn" Holt, Dan Mandis, Dewayne McDaniels, and Lisa Medel. I'm sure their Fridays are a lot less hectic (and less fattening) since "Pester Ray" quit coming down. I also appreciate Dr. Lew Bishop for all of his encouragement and support.

The office secretary here at the Church of Christ of Hesperia, Kathy Schrecengost, kept me on a relatively even keel throughout this whole writing process. She prevented a lot of my ministerial work from falling through the cracks while I labored both to complete the book and pay attention to my regular duties. My thanks to Joyce Haggard for supplying the transcript database and Kari Hartwick for helping so diligently with the topical research.

I'm also indebted to the kindness of my friends and colleagues, who made several contributions to these pages.

My heartfelt gratitude to all the folks at Chariot Victor, who

9

truly have the patience of saints. Especially to Lee Hough, who saw my idea on the Web, saw something a little worthwhile in it, and worked so hard to make this book happen. Thank you for not giving up on me. I can't really put into words how much all the encouragement and help you've provided means to me. I truly appreciate the hard labor everyone at Chariot Victor has had to endure to give birth to this first-time author. May our next book be less eventful.

And many thanks to my wife, Linda, and my children, Jason, Justin, Jessica, and Jarrod, for their support and encouragement, even though the last several months has taken its toll.

I couldn't have done this without any of you.

Ray McClendon

Foreword

by

Dr. Laura C. Schlessinger

Tens of millions of listeners to the "Dr. Laura Schlessinger Program" have heard me humorously and affectionately proclaim Ray McClendon as "My Favorite Pastor." Our relationship began with a number of faxes Pastor Ray would send me during my broadcast. My audience and I would enjoy the fun in his whimsical poems and musings, as well as contemplate the profundities in his more serious pieces dealing with spirituality and character. I found a "soul brother" both in his philosophy and in his passion for righteousness, integrity, and accountability.

After publishing a number of his contributions in my *Dr. Laura Perspective* magazine, we finally met at one of my outdoor broadcast and book signings in Arrowhead, California. Was I ever stunned to see him—and not just because it was a (welcome) surprise, but because I never imagined that such a clever, serious, religious minister would appear on a motorcycle! Being a "closet Harley mama," I figured ours was a friendship made in heaven!

While I was working on my book *The Ten Commandments— The Significance of God's Laws in Everyday Life*, I consulted Ray for a Christian position on a certain issue. I waited anxiously for one or two succinct paragraphs summarizing Jesus' teachings on this position. If I remember correctly, he sent me some twenty, single-spaced pages, exhaustively covering the subject. I was impressed with his thoughtfulness and desire to make sure that I had the whole picture. He is truly a gentleman and a scholar.

I trust and respect Ray as a friend, a father, and as a clergyman. When I read his many spontaneous essays supporting my positions on moral behavior and responsibility, bringing forth biblical verses to document his thinking, I was impressed with the possibilities of a bridge between my Orthodox Jewish perspective and his serious Christian perspective. Our interaction demonstrated that those who are serious about their faith, though they may be of different religious persuasions, are more of like mind than people usually imagine—getting caught up as folks do, in issues of divisiveness rather than synergy.

I never think of my program as entertainment, nor my work as a job. I consider these efforts a mission. In Hebrew, the phrase *Tikkun Olam* means to "perfect the world." Serious Jews accept as a blessing the responsibility to live and work in such a way as to help perfect God's world. This is the perspective my family has adopted. This point of view has brought much peace, meaning, and purpose to our lives. I believe that Pastor Ray McClendon's life and work is a blessing to God and does much to help perfect this world. This book is yet one more gift he is giving.

Dr. Laura Schlessinger
AKA "My Kid's Mom"
Los Angeles, 1999

Introduction

Early one morning in late February 1997, I was observing my morning coffee ritual when the church secretary poked her head in my office and said, "Telephone—it's Dr. Laura!" While I had talked with Dr. Laura Schlessinger a couple of times before (in connection with an article I had written for her magazine), a phone conversation with this prominent radio talk show host could hardly be considered routine. So as the butterflies in my stomach began to flap, I took a deep breath, willed them to at least fly in formation, and picked up the extension.

Dr. Laura was calling to ask if I might be interested in writing a book that would look at her show from a Christian perspective—a biblical perspective that would include principles from both Old and New Testaments.

I articulately replied, "Uh . . . er . . . uh . . ."

"Let me guess," she said, "you're terrified."

I helpfully nodded yes.

Saying things on the phone that stun people—leave them speechlessly groping for an intelligent response—is one of Dr. Laura's specialties, her stock-in-trade. It happens all the time on her radio program. Callers spend two or three minutes laying out their "incredibly complex and tortured moral dilemma," and she cuts to the chase with, "Just tell the truth!" Stark silence ensues; then, after a long pause, the caller repeats her statement, "Just tell the truth'? Mmmm . . . I never thought of that!"

Now I knew how her callers felt. I'd never thought of writing a book about Dr. Laura. But here she was asking me to think about it, and here I was stammering incoherently like an idiot. Fortunately, Dr. Laura "knows the feeling," so she was understanding. She offered a few words of encouragement, and I told her I'd think about it and expressed my appreciation for the invitation, which was as gracious as it was unexpected. Then it was over—the most surreal telephone conversation I'd ever had.

Obviously, I decided to take the plunge.

In Search of Intelligent Life on AM Radio

I began to listen to Dr. Laura's radio program about six years ago. It was late at night, and I was fighting to stay awake while on my way to Tucson, Arizona. I was channel surfing the AM band to see what kind of nonsense was currently wafting o'er the airwaves, when the channel seeker zeroed in on a pleasant voice that was in the midst of this monologue on . . . *morality?* Did I hear right? Someone was taking a stand on morality on AM radio, and it wasn't even *religious programming?* How on earth did *she* get on the radio? How on earth does she *stay* on the radio? At first I was curious, then intrigued, and, finally, hooked. It took only one show, as I recall. Here was someone who pulled no punches. Someone who got right into people's faces to make them see the truth about themselves and the situation they were in. Someone who made sense.

She not only offered legitimate counsel to nearly every caller, she could actually be profound. How many other radio talk show hosts held people accountable for their choices, decisions, and actions—and, incredibly, even cited a biblical principle or included God in the solution to the problem? Dr. Laura insisted that character, courage, and conscience really did matter. I was amazed! Still am.

So, like millions of others in America and abroad, I became a faithful listener. More often than not over the past six years, I've kept the radio in my office tuned in to her show. In my line of work as a Christian minister, listening to Dr. Laura does not constitute a distraction; it's on-the-job training! The vast majority of problems that require my counsel relate to problems either in the family or between members of the congregation. They invariably stem from people's lack of love, respect, and spirituality. Since folks are folks everywhere you go, those issues are found in the average Dr. Laura caller as well. Consequently, I've learned a great deal about how to more effectively listen and respond to people by listening to Dr. Laura.

Since the questions, answers, and monologues on her show frequently cover religious territory, I suppose it was inevitable that I started to send her faxes. It was hard to resist, because I would often be reading about or studying the same issue she was commenting on. Since we also share a basically conservative point of view on many things and have a similar sense of humor (subtle, a little dry, and slightly absurd at times), I soon found myself including political commentary, religious content, various and sundry current events, whimsical poetry, and just plain funny stuff in the fax mix. Whatever I collected for my own use, I'd just clip and fax to Dr. Laura.

Evidently, she appreciates the material as much as I do, given the number of pieces she has read on the air. She has come to refer to me on occasion as her "fax buddy from Hesperia." Sending material to her over the past four years has led to friendship and has also provided some new forums—her magazine, Web site, and now this book—in which I get to occasionally express some views that, I hope, are helpful and worthwhile.

What You May Expect from This Book

Just what does a short, orthodox, Jewish, female radio talk show host who has an extensive, formal, East Coast education have in common with a tall, conservative, Christian, male minister who has a nonextensive, informal, West Coast education? The Judeo-Christian Bible.

True, her faith centers in the Old Testament (though she also studies the New Testament), and mine centers in the New Testament (though I also study the Old Testament). But the bottom line for us is that the Scriptures, both Old and New Testaments, are capable of steering people toward God, who made each of us in His image.

Over the years, Dr. Laura has grown increasingly spiritual and knowledgeable about religious matters, and her show reflects that. She looks to Scripture more and more as a place for her and everyone else to hang their hats, because it provides an objective moral standard. The Scriptures can instruct us in forming the kind of character that can solve the lion's share of our problems—at least, the ones we are personally responsible for.

As a Christian preacher, I rely on and point others to the Scriptures too. I do so because of what they are and who is behind them:

> All Scripture is God-breathed and is useful for teaching, rebuking, correcting and training in righteousness, so that the man of God may be thoroughly equipped for every good work. (2 Timothy 3:16-17)

So, Dr. Laura and I share a common ethical standard from which we derive the same basic moral and family values. And we both try to promote these values at every opportunity. We may have different mediums and a different audience, but much of our message is the same. Yes, she's Jewish and I'm Christian. We have distinct and important differences—but we also have distinct and important similarities. Our biggest problem in American society today is not that we have too many sincere people of faith who are divided on theological issues; our biggest problem is that we don't have enough people who sincerely live out the divinely inspired truths of the Judeo-Christian Bible. The single greatest casualty in all of this has been the family, the foundation—the core—of our society. After that, a loss of community. A mutual caring for one another not just because we share a national heritage, but because we share humanity.

In my mind, one of the single greatest services Dr. Laura has provided for our country is that she keeps the primacy of family and the importance of community on the front burners of her moral health show. The vast majority of callers have moral dilemmas that are keyed to relationships. Coworker relationships. Dating relationships. Neighbor relationships. Most of all, family relationships. If you listen closely, the majority of "testimonials" or kudos she receives revolve around what her counsel has done for their families. "I am my kid's mom . . . I am my kid's dad" are now part of our national vocabulary.

If you do not currently believe in God or use the Bible as a blueprint for living, I hope this book will give you some food for thought and motivate you to take a serious look at both. If you already profess faith (give intellectual and verbal assent to God and the Judeo-Christian Scriptures), my prayer is that you will examine the quality of your profession and see if you are really taking your faith seriously. Does your belief in God make a real difference in your life, or are you just whistling spiritual Dixie?

Like many of you, I have read polls that talk about our "Christian" nation—how a vast majority of our citizens still believe in God and how most still go to church. But I must be honest here. When I'm on the streets every day—on the freeways, in stores and places of business, dropping my kids off at school, etc.—I'm wondering, *Where are all those people?* I know what a lot of people claim to believe, but obviously there's a big difference between intellectual assent and a living, breathing faith that affects your life and your behavior in tangible ways. Dr. Laura correctly points out that only a relatively small minority in any given religion practice their faith with sincerity, devotion, and fidelity to godly principles.

One caller, for example, once asked for some advice about what to do with a Sunday School teacher who, in her opinion, held some strange views. Dr. Laura did her best to nail down exactly what the problem was. But as the conversation progressed, it became increasingly clear that the caller had more of a personal ax to grind than legitimate reasons for concern. After hanging up, Dr. Laura made the following observation:

> Mmmm, sounds like someone wanted to be mad, wanted to be exclusionary—all without any information that something bad was actually happening. Which, ya know, I hate to nag (that's a lie), *but* if you call yourself a Jew or a Christian . . . you darn well better behave that way when you call me, because we don't do "in name only" stuff around here. We do an actual behavior. People ask me all the time why I decided to write a book on the Ten Commandments. One of the reasons is that everybody walks around saying they are moral, they are Jewish, they

are Christian, they're this, they're that. But you ask them exactly what that means, and they don't have an answer. What are the Ten Commandments? Uh . . . most people can get through three, and not in any order. So we say we are and we say we do, but you know something? We don't back it up real well. And *that* is why I'm nagging.

When I heard the good doctor point this out, I was reminded of something Jesus emphasized. The Lord reserved His most stinging rebukes for those who merely professed to be religious—the religious hypocrites of His day.

> Then Jesus said to the crowds and to his disciples: "The teachers of the law and the Pharisees sit in Moses' seat. So you must obey them and do everything they tell you. But do not do what they do, for they do not practice what they preach. . . .
>
> "Woe to you, teachers of the law and Pharisees, you hypocrites! You give a tenth of your spices—mint, dill and cummin. But you have neglected the more important matters of the law—justice, mercy and faithfulness. You should have practiced the latter, without neglecting the former. . . .
>
> "Woe to you, teachers of the law and Pharisees, you hypocrites! You are like whitewashed tombs, which look beautiful on the outside but on the inside are full of dead men's bones and everything unclean." (Matthew 23:1-3, 23, 27)

I spent a number of years in the cemetery industry before I entered the ministry, and believe me, no one appreciates the analogy Jesus used more than I do. When Jesus uses the grave and speaks of exterior beauty and internal corruption, He is expressing just how *disgusted* He really is with hypocrisy and misplaced priorities, especially with those who ought to know better!

The prophet Micah in the Old Testament expressed the futility of an empty profession that manifested itself through insincere religious worship. Would a thousand sacrificial rams or ten thousand rivers of oil constitute an acceptable sacrifice? Not if your heart isn't right. Religious observance has never been an end in itself; it is the means to greater spirituality—a sincere faith that will kindle proper behavior toward God and everybody else.

> He has showed you, O man, what is good.
> And what does the Lord require of you?
> To act justly and to love mercy and to walk humbly with
> your God. (Micah 6:8)

Unfortunately, the simple truth is that many religious folks are what they are more in name than in substance. Much of their worship and churchgoin' is just so much ritual ceremony, void of true love and devotion. That is why their lives are filled with problems and their relationships are greatly troubled.

So, don't expect this book to be a comparison of Judaism and Christianity. That's not what it is about. Don't expect to read on these pages an analysis of what I think Dr. Laura does wrong; she already has plenty of critics and detractors. My desire is to stand shoulder-to-shoulder with her and lift my voice with hers to everyone who will listen: You need God in your life, you need a sincere faith based on an objective moral standard, and you need to practice that. For those already professing faith in God and the Judeo-Christian Scriptures, I want to encourage you to really get on the stick and start practicing what you are preaching.

Consider how popular Dr. Laura's program has become: 20 million listeners per week. Consider that the main reason she has become so popular is because her show is a genuine help to those who listen to her on a regular basis. Now consider how Bible-based her show has become in the last five years. What does that say? Doesn't that tell us that if Dr. Laura is helpful, it is because the Bible is helpful? That if Dr. Laura's advice is perceived as wise and good, it is because biblical principles are wise and good? That if Dr. Laura's nagging yields practical benefits for listeners, it is because biblical ethics themselves are exceedingly practical? And doesn't this all, then, emphasize the importance of Scripture as well as a closer, more vibrant relationship with God?

When more of our neighbors, more of our coworkers, more of the people we simply pass on the street, and more of *us* begin to pursue the ethics presented in the Bible within our own families and communities, we will all find a significantly richer, more satisfying life. Our families will become more closely knit together in love. Our communities will be stronger. Our country overall will be more united and more peaceful. It is this that enables me to take my "literary stand" with Dr. Laura in the writing of this book, and I count it a great privilege and honor to be able to do so.

The Appeal of Dr. Laura

Dear Dr. Laura,
This letter is to thank you for the knock upside the head . . .
thank you for your wisdom, your humor, and your uncanny
ability to cut to the chase. I think you're an angel sent by the
divine saints in heaven to help us cure our pain and proceed
with dignity.

*—Letter from a woman who had just left her hus-
band and was heading for a hotel. On the way, she
heard Dr. Laura taking a woman to task for
blaming her husband when she was the one who
had "changed the rules" in her marriage. Seeing
herself in that conversation, she made a U-turn to
her husband's office and asked for his forgiveness.*

A Mother in Israel She was a woman for the times. Her
name meant "honeybee" or simply
"bee," which was an appropriate name, considering the systematic
and diligent way in which she worked to help ensure the spiritual
health and survival of her people. She lived in the hill country of
Ephraim, and many were the children of Israel who journeyed to
that well-known palm tree where she could be found. We know her
as Deborah, from the Old Testament book of Judges, chapters 4–5.
She was one of ancient Israel's most courageous leaders.

Deborah stepped onto the scene during a time of great tur-
moil. People struggled with their problems; the entire nation was
diminished because the people were moving away from God and
goodness. It was a time when, as it's repeated throughout the latter
chapters of Judges, "Everyone did what was right in his own eyes."
People faced numerous "moral dilemmas," so they began to seek
the counsel of a woman who called them to have faith in God and

to live according to His divine standard.

Strong moral leadership was in short supply in her day. As a prophetess of God, she ably judged the matters the people brought before her, showing them how to apply the statutes and principles of the Law of Moses in their daily lives. Unfortunately, Deborah did not have a lot of help among the other leaders. This became clear when she summoned a fellow named Barak. God commanded him to take ten thousand men and go toward Mount Tabor to confront their Canaanite oppressors. There God would defeat Sisera, the captain of the enemy army, and Israel would be victorious. When Barak wimpishly said he would go *only* if Deborah went with him, she agreed but told him, "The honor will not be yours, for the Lord will hand Sisera over to a woman." (Who nailed him good!)

In praising God for His victory, Deborah was as quick to express sincere praise for those who finally exercised much-needed leadership as she was to unflinchingly confront those tribes who shirked their responsibility (Judges 5:12-18). Deborah was not a woman with whom you wanted to cross swords.

In her song of tribute to God, Deborah said, "Village life in Israel ceased, ceased until I, Deborah, arose, arose a mother in Israel" (v. 7). In other words, Israel's peaceful and prosperous way of life came to a halt when the Canaanite oppressors gained the upper hand against the Israelites. That sad situation wasn't going to change until the people turned from their evil ways and began to live the kind of lives God had called them to. God used Deborah, a mother in Israel, to accomplish that. It was an appropriate metaphor because she, like all good mothers, was hardworking and wise. She called her "children" to strength, courage, morality, and dignity. She held them strictly accountable for their choices and actions. She honored those who responded. She chided those who didn't.

| **A Mother in America** | Any of this sound familiar? If so, it's probably because, thousands of years |

later, smack-dab in the middle of Western civilization, is another Jewish woman who dwells beneath her own 50,000-watt "palm tree."

Her countrypeople, too, come to her daily to enlist the counsel of a wise and moral woman who holds forth faith in God and belief in an objective and divine standard to help get lives back on track. And when caller after caller after caller begin their conversations with statements like, "Dr. Laura, you have made *such* a difference in my life. . . . I (we) are so grateful for what you stand for. . . . You have been so much help to us. . . . You've done so much good"—it bears eloquent testimony to the effectiveness of her daily polemic. She, too, laments apathy and corruption in high places. She, too, excoriates slackers and shirkers. She, too, is quick to praise and honor all who are willing to take a stand and do what's right. She, too, calls it as she sees it.

And like the people in Deborah's day, we, too, live in a time "when everyone does what's right in his own eyes." When spiritual, moral leaders like Deborah are scarce, and Baraks are everywhere. We live in a time of wickedness, with all the uncertainty, doubt, pessimism, confusion, and heartache it brings. Many have lost their way philosophically and spiritually; behavioral anarchy seems to be the order of the day. So when people are fortunate enough to stumble across Dr. Laura's program, to hear someone stand up for simple decency and honor, they wind up staying a good, long while. It's encouraging to hear someone "out in the trenches," outside of our churches, speaking bravely and tirelessly of character, courage, and conscience. Millions of people are encouraged to know that, day after day, there is someplace they can go to hear the truth of an objective, moral standard brought to bear on the difficult problems we all share. One cannot make such a lovely difference in so many people's lives and not gain a devoted following.

I do not believe that Dr. Laura is literally a prophetess of God, though I do believe God is doing a lot of good work in and through her. She is neither perfect nor infallible, and she doesn't claim to be. But here's the thing. What Dr. Laura and her program are mainly about is calling people to become more accountable for their actions. To stand up and take responsibility for themselves. To have faith in God and follow His standard of truth. To live better, richer, and fuller lives by being less selfish and more devoted to their families, churches, and communities. To be more upright people in general. I'm all for that! Aren't you?

Dr. Laura accomplishes her daily task with the common sense that comes from experience—"Hey, I wasn't born this age!" she reminds her listeners. From the passion that comes from strong conviction—"I'm serious about religion . . . I'm serious about getting you serious about your religion!" And from the virtues rooted in an objective standard of morality that has stood the test of time and that speaks to the hearts and needs of people everywhere.

Sydney Smith, English clergyman and writer from the early nineteenth century said, "Great men hallow a whole people, and lift up all who live in their time." That is why this tiny woman is such a giant in so many of our eyes. She lifts up all who listen to her.

What's Your Moral Dilemma?

"Hi! I'm Dr. Laura Schlessinger. My number is 1-800-D-R-L-A-(pause)-U-R-A, and we try to determine right from wrong on *this* program. . . ."

Carolyn Holt, who produces Dr. Laura's program and screens her calls, preps telephonic hopefuls with that purpose in mind: "Here at the 'Dr. Laura Show,' we try to help callers figure out what's right and what's wrong regarding their moral behavior. Now fill in the blank for me. Is it right or wrong for me to do . . . *what?* Is it right or is it wrong for me to do or not do . . . *this or that?*" She varies it a little, but the bottom line is to get callers to think about their "issue" in terms of morality.

Care to guess what one of the most frequent responses to Carolyn's question is? "What do you mean by *moral?*" Hmmm . . . isn't that amazing? Concepts regarding right and wrong are becoming so relative and obscure that people have difficulty communicating their problems in that context. I've listened to Cousin Carolyn as she works, and this inability is one of the greatest challenges she has in screening Dr. Laura's phone calls. *What is the moral dilemma here?*

A dilemma, according to the *American Heritage Dictionary*, is "A situation that requires a choice between options that are mutually exclusive." A moral dilemma, then, would require a choice between something either immoral or moral. You don't get more mutually exclusive than that!

Animals are value-neutral. They do not operate within the sphere of morality. When they kill for food, or when males mate with the first available female or multiple females, there's no morality or immorality involved—only instinctive behavior. You can teach an animal to do or not do something, but you cannot teach it why. Animals do not have moral dilemmas (not even cats!).

However, when we as human beings cater to our fleshly lusts without regard to what is considered moral (what we often call our animal side), it's not an issue of *amorality*, it's a matter of *immorality*. That's because we are consciously and willfully rejecting that which elevates us above the animal kingdom. We are saying no to God and, consequently, dishonoring Him.

You see, we have both a moral and volitional component that animals, by their very nature, do not have. We have this *by our very nature*—another aspect of what it means to be made in the image of God. We are morally aware. We have a sense of right and wrong. Dr. Laura drives this point home constantly, because until people really start believing it they won't begin to see the need to live in a morally upright way. They won't accept responsibility for behaving badly. And they won't realize that they have the will to do one or the other.

These differences are worth noting because too many people today are "acting like animals." And that is a genuine tragedy, because when we act like animals, we actually behave much worse than they do. When morality fails, we have no instinct to serve as a "governor" and we do far more damage to ourselves and our world than animals ever could.

"Knowing Good and Evil"

Jesus referred to humankind's inherent moral nature when He taught that "man does not live by bread alone . . ."

(Matthew 4:4). He did not mean that we must have peanut butter, jelly, and a glass of milk; He was speaking of our dual nature. We are flesh *and* spirit. There is more to life than just meeting one's physical needs.

Genesis 1:26 tells us that God said, "Let us make man in our image, in our likeness, and let them rule over the fish of the sea and the birds of the air, over the livestock, over all the earth, and over all the creatures that move along the ground." The dominion God calls us to exercise over the animal kingdom reflects our close kinship with God and emphasizes the important differences between human beings and animals. Like animals, we have a fleshly nature. Like God, we have a spiritual nature as well as a moral awareness. After Adam and Eve ate the fruit from the tree of the knowledge of good and evil, God said, "The man has now become like one of us, knowing good and evil" (Genesis 3:22).

It's that "knowing good and evil" part that plays such a huge role in Dr. Laura's counsel. She strongly suggests (and at times even demands) that her listeners think about things in a moral context. She made this statement to a young woman who was shacking up and didn't have a "moral handle" on the implications of living that way:

> You don't need to be human to have sex and to cuddle. The thing about being human is that we have this great potential to elevate ourselves way above the animals and hold certain things holy. That's where the morality comes in, in deciding if we are going to behave closer to termites or farther away from termites. So right now, you've been living like a termite. Do you want to elevate yourself? If so, you have to elevate your thinking first.

This is such a tremendous part of Dr. Laura's appeal—simply to get folks thinking about the morality of their behavior. To see that right and wrong have a lot more to do with the problems in their lives than "psychological issues."

| **The Monologues** | One of the most stimulating and educa-tional aspects of Dr. Laura's program is |

how she begins each hour of her show. She underscores the principles dealt with in her conversations with callers by linking them with current events and other relevant tidbits gleaned from her own reading and as well as from her handy-dandy fax machine (which she calls her "aorta"). Listeners from all over the country send her reams of material from which she selects the funniest, most touching, and most insightful pieces to share with her audience. Whatever touches on morality in individual lives or our educational, religious, or political institutions is grist for Dr. Laura's monologue mill.

The Humor

As Solomon wrote, "A cheerful heart is good medicine" (Proverbs 17:22). Humor is a frequent guest on Dr. Laura's program and livens things up quite a bit. For the last several years, she has conducted her now famous (or infamous) Thanksgiving Corny Joke Show. Since her show is, for the most part, rather serious in nature, the chuckles are a welcome respite and help keep her and her listeners sane.

Her favorite kind of humor is related to the Bible and children. A couple of times she has even solicited some from me during the broadcast—"Pastor Ray, if you're listening now, please send me some more biblical stuff . . . or things about kids, all right?" As a matter of fact, it is with some irony that I note that our own fax correspondence really had its beginning, well, "In the beginning. . . ."

It had been a sillier week than usual due to a proliferation of plucky poultry persiflage (chicken jokes). Once they began streaming off the fax, they began to dominate the spots between callers and the monologues until, later on in the week, she chortled, "Enough already! It's been fun, but let's get on with other things, shall we? *No more chicken jokes!*" But I thought, *Just one more.* I figured she'd read a religious chicken joke, but it'd have to be good. Since she's Jewish, I decided to relate it to the Old Testament. *Let's see . . . Genesis . . . the Fall of humanity . . .* and the joke just popped into my head. The next day during one of her breaks, Dr. Laura said, "OK! One more chicken joke. For this one we have to go all the way back to Genesis. Why did the very first chicken cross the road? Because the Lord God said, 'Thou shalt not cross the road, for in the day thou crossest the road, thou shalt surely fry!'" (Isn't it amazing how we're often not tempted to do something until it's forbidden?)

My wife received an "I Am My Kid's Mom" T-shirt out of that, plus it was read again at that year's corny joke show. I figure that made me winner, if unofficially, of the Chicken Joke of the Year Award—and darn proud of it!

The Pathos

Our funny bones aren't the only emotional buttons pressed during Dr. Laura's monologues. When she says to get the tissues out, you'd better listen, because you will likely need them. The following is a typical example:

> I'm not going to identify the person who wrote me, because it is not relevant. But this is what he wrote. "The news today is filled with people and events that have gone wrong in this world. I'm writing to you to tell you about someone who made good with his life. My father lived his life as if you had scripted it. He devoted himself to his wife for forty-seven years. He has eight children and seventeen grandchildren. Although he was a very successful businessman, this was not his main focus. He provided my brothers, my sister, and myself an opportunity to enter the medical profession. He was the strong force in our making the decision to enter this field. Our upbringing was rooted in firm religious convictions. He was a man with unwavering moral values. My father died this past week. It was a huge blow to my family and our city. On his deathbed I was hoping . . ."
>
> (*Dr. Laura:* Up to now you've heard this before, right? Wait until you hear this. Get your tissues or your sleeves ready.)
>
> ". . . my father would provide me with a final statement on the meaning of life. He did not. After he died I

questioned my brother about this. His answer was simple. The meaning of life was not in some final statement my father could have made, *but rather in the way he lived his life.* (Dr. Laura's voice trembles as she reads the last sentence). *The meaning of life was our family.*"

Okay . . . I'm trying so hard not to sniffle . . . (sniffle, sniffle). I so appreciate it when you share such insights with me.

Don't think tears aren't streaming down faces all over the country when Dr. Laura shares things like that. A member of our congregation came into my office one day when I was blubbering and blowing my nose, and he asked with a face etched deeply with concern, "What's wrong, Ray?" He thought something terrible had just happened. I just waved my hand and said, "Oh, it's Dr. Laura's fault!"

Something spiritual, something scriptural and good is happening when we laugh and cry along with Dr. Laura and each other. In the Apostle Paul's instructions to the Christian community at Rome, he gave the following admonitions:

> Love must be sincere. Hate what is evil; cling to what is good. Be devoted to one another in brotherly love. Honor one another above yourselves. Never be lacking in zeal, but keep your spiritual fervor, serving the Lord. Be joyful in hope, patient in affliction, faithful in prayer. Share with God's people who are in need. Practice hospitality.
>
> Bless those who persecute you; bless and do not curse. Rejoice with those who rejoice; mourn with those who mourn. (Romans 12:9-15)

One of the most profound principles in Paul's words is the counsel to rejoice with and weep for one another. We realize we do not turn our emotions off and on like a faucet—Paul was not suggesting that at all. What makes it possible to share in the rejoicing and weeping of other people is the cultivation of a strong, mutual affinity. In the absence of brotherly love—and the sincere care and concern that springs from it—it is impossible to be moved by what moves others.

I learned what Paul meant in Romans 12:15 in 1980. A lesson I'll never forget. Mount Saint Helens had just erupted. I walked into a convenience store and, while standing in line, noted a picture on the cover of one of the news magazines. It was one of the bleakest scenes I'd ever beheld. Though miles from the volcano, the ash had turned everything monochrome. The trees were gray. The street was gray. The buildings were gray. The pickup truck in the center of the photo was gray. Even the dead body of that poor little boy lying in the back of that truck who had smothered to death on volcanic ash was gray.

After shaking my head and muttering the obligatory "too bad" under my breath, I stepped forward to make my purchases, wisecracked with the clerk, and left—my mind already occupied with "more important things." A couple of weeks later when I was trying to make sense of Romans 12:15, that picture came back to haunt me. Why wasn't I bothered more by it? Why wasn't I more saddened? How could I so callously and easily dismiss it from my thinking and my conscience? What if he had been my little boy?

Ouch. That last question answered all of the others. We rejoice and weep with those to whom we are close. That is Paul's point. God is calling us to the kinds of caring behaviors that help develop strong and loving relationships. A sense of community begins with a felt kinship. God makes it clear that He desires and intends for us to live in this fashion—although He does not force us to.

Right, wrong, and the difference they make in family and community life have become the main course of Dr. Laura's daily fare. She communicates clearly that how we learn to live with one another is the most important thing. Not stuff. Not things. Not possessions. But people.

One of the most valuable insights about the importance of living life within strong families and closely knit communities came to me years ago as a young man. I was engaged in the most boring job in cemetery work, edging the markers or headstones. Because there are thousands of them, it's a tedious task that I would often try to make more interesting by musing over the many different epitaphs I would read.

One afternoon, it dawned on me what all of those epitaphs really meant. Except for the occasional picture or emblem that would speak of a particular hobby or accomplishment, virtually every epitaph I read spoke to the surpassing importance of family. *Beloved wife and mother. Beloved husband and father. Precious son or daughter. In our hearts you live still. Gone but not forgotten. We miss you so much.* And on and on they went.

You don't see epitaphs that talk about what a great secretary this one was or what a great salesman that one was or what a nice BMW this one drove or how many corporate jets that one had. They don't speak of hairstyles or fashion. They don't speak of houses and bank accounts. They speak of life lived in intimate and loving relationships and the hope that someday we will all meet again.

The Wisdom

One listener faxed in the following marvelous—and true—story, which Dr. Laura read on the air. Its poignant truths teach us much about seeing ourselves and others the way God sees us and about treating one another with care and dignity. I used it as the main illustration in a sermon I preached titled "The Importance of Our Humanity." The main scriptural text I used was the book of Jonah, and I suggested to the congregation that there was an important reason Jonah did not feel the same way about the Ninevites as God did. He saw them differently than God did. He did not have the pathos God had for them. God truly loved and cared for those people despite their lovelessness, selfishness, and wickedness. They were His creation, after all. But they were not Jonah's, and Jonah lacked the spirituality to appreciate or care for or respect them for their common humanity. We all wrestle with this problem, and most of our troubles have everything to do with this.

A sensitive and loving mother had discovered pornographic literature behind the dresser in her young teenage son's room while helping him clean. She set it aside without comment while they finished the room, giving herself time to think through her approach—a wise decision. Finally, she sat down with him and, to his horror, began to thumb through the pictures. She came to one crass nude photo after another and made statements like "*This* is somebody's sister. *This* is somebody's daughter. Is *this* how you picture me in my bedroom? Is *this* what you would want your sister doing?" When she had finished thoroughly "tweaking" his perspective (by humbling him, embarrassing him, and really making him think), she had him throw the magazine in the garbage with the admonition to never bring that trash into her home again.

What had she done? She had *humanized* the women in that magazine. She tried to get her son to attach a certain amount of worth and dignity to the women by viewing them as he would those for whom he cared, rather than viewing them simply as things to be used to gratify his own selfish lust. In fact, she had given them more dignity than they had given themselves.

A few years later, when the young man returned from a trip to Nevada with some college buddies, he came to see his mother. As they sat down to visit, he began to tell her about the trip, which included a visit to a brothel. She interrupted him with a serious expression on her face, saying, "Some things a mother just does not need to know." Her son, however, insisted that it was something he had to tell her about.

So as she sat in somber silence, he talked about how they all had psyched themselves up to go into this place and each had then proceeded to "pick his girl." Next thing you know, he's in this room by himself for a time, and while he's in there he notices that her room is decorated just like a little girl's room "at home." He notices a family picture on the dresser and thinks to himself, "Oh no, this girl is somebody's daughter." Then he spies another picture on the wall and thinks, "Oh no, this girl is somebody's sister!" When the prostitute came into the room and asked what she could do for him, he said something to the effect that he had a headache. "Could you just give me a neck rub?" he asked.

Later, in the car, all the guys were crowing about their activities while the young man sat silently. When they asked him about his experiences, he told them what he'd done and why—and proceeded to give them his mother's lecture. "Mom," he said, "they sat in dead silence after that, and no one said a word for the next twenty miles."

With what must have been a proud heart, this mother thanked her son for sharing that with her. "After all," she said, "there are some things a mother just needs to know."

Our country would be so much better off if we could learn to look at others as God does. If we could see our family, friends—everybody—as creatures of infinite value because we are all made in the image of God.

Not Your Average National Mom

One of the criticisms often leveled at Dr. Laura is that she is too blunt, too harsh—even to the point of being rude. Ironically, I have learned over time that her unapologetic directness is actually a large part of her appeal. Others have noted this as well.

Anita Manning, in *USA Today*, asked, "Now, with fewer nuns around and Mom off at work, to whom can we turn for a good lambasting when we need it? To Dr. Laura." She later notes in the same article that her "on-air style is tough, abrasive, confrontational."[1]

Arsenio Orteza, in an article he wrote for *World Magazine* about Dr. Laura, notes the same characteristics and offers this explanation: "If she is tougher than such past 'national moms' as Harriet Nelson or Florence Henderson, these are different times. Her consistent opposition to abortion, 'shacking up,' divorce, and other manifestations of self-centeredness has made her refreshingly impatient with illogic and equivocation. Callers expecting a therapist whose main mannerism is a sympathetically nodding head get an awakening that, by today's touchy-feely standards, may seem rude."[2]

When people ask her why she is so blunt, she points out that she only has two to three minutes to make her point. She doesn't have time to fiddle around. The kid-glove approach usually doesn't get the job done (though she uses it when appropriate). Her goal is to plant a relevant moral seed that she hopes will germinate, grow, and eventually flourish both in the caller's life and in the lives of all who are listening. Not only is that exactly what many of her callers need, it is a part of what her listening audience appreciates about her.

Callers to whom she has read "the riot act" have written or faxed her the next day to tell her how upset they were when they hung up; but after thinking about it, they realized she was right. If it hadn't been for her getting in their faces, they wouldn't have gotten the point. The following example is one of many I have read:

> Dear Dr. Laura,
>
> I'm certain that you've heard my story before; I must admit that when I first began listening to your program, I used to become angry. I thought that you were too harsh in your responses. As I listened more, it felt like the revelation I discovered with my own parents. As *I* got older, *they* got smarter! The more I listened to you, the more I recognized that your experience has enabled you to wade through the "bull" and get to the point! I am a person who needs to sometimes be met head-on and told things in a very matter-of-fact way. . . . I appreciate your candidness.

So the next time you hear Dr. Laura's bluntness, just close your eyes and imagine a mom wagging her finger at her wayward child, who needs to "be told a thing or two." I suspect you'll find that her tone will suddenly sound familiar.

| **The Bottom Line** | Twenty million people listen to "Mother Laura," as she's been dubbed, and profit

from the principles she teaches because those principles help them find their way back to being the right kind of husband, wife, father, mother, child, etc. It's important, then, for them (and the rest of our nation) to learn that these principles are rooted in the Judeo-Christian Bible.

Dr. Laura is effective because the Bible is effective. That's why she is always encouraging—even demanding, as Deborah did—people to turn back to faith in God and the divine standard we've received from Him. And *that* is why her words help cure our pain and help us proceed with dignity.

Character, Courage, and Conscience

Do not merely listen to the word, and so deceive yourselves. Do what it says. Anyone who listens to the word but does not do what it says is like a man who looks at his face in the mirror and, after looking at himself, goes away and immediately forgets what he looks like. But the man who looks intently into the perfect law that gives freedom, and continues to do this, not forgetting what he has heard, but doing it—he will be blessed in what he does.

James, circa A.D. 50, Israel

You are not what you say you are; you are not what you would like to be, or what you think you ought to be. You are exactly what you do.

Dr. Laura, circa A.D. 1996, Hartford, Connecticut

| **Ethos and Character** | Moral or immoral, virtuous or evil, good or bad, the best measure of a |

person's character is what a person says and does. As Jesus told us in the Sermon on the Mount, "By their fruit you will recognize them" (Matthew 7:16). It is foolish to believe something will come out of a person that's not already in there. Dr. Kenneth McFarland, in his book *Eloquence in Public Speaking*, observes, "What is in the well of a person's heart will show up in the bucket of his speech."[1] We could adjust that slightly to read, "What is in the well of people's hearts will show up in the bucket of their lives." The Bible teaches both: "As water reflects a face, so a man's heart reflects the man" (Proverbs 27:19).

Character is synonymous with morality, because our character is formed and shaped according to the morality we embrace (or fail to embrace). Character is also synonymous with ethics, because our character is seen in the ethics we practice (or fail to practice). In fact, our English word *ethical* derives from the Greek word *ethikos*, which comes from *ethos*, which means *character*. *Ethos* is also translated throughout the New Testament as *habit, manner,* and *custom*.

So . . . what are your habits? What do you customarily do day in and day out? How does it affect your relationships in your family and with your neighbors and coworkers? There's your character. As Jesus taught then and as Dr. Laura preaches, teaches, and nags today, "What you *do* demonstrates what you *are!*" Dozens of Dr. Laura's listeners have faxed the following piece of prose to her. The author may be anonymous, but the truth is timeless.

> Watch your thoughts; they become words.
> Watch your words; they become actions.
> Watch your actions, they become habits.
> Watch your habits; they become character.
> Watch your character; it becomes your destiny.

The reason character has taken center stage on Dr. Laura's show is because it has gone AWL *(absent with leave)* in our society. It is disappearing from public life because it has left family life. As Michael Josephson, founder of the Josephson Institute of Ethics, has observed, "The hole in our moral ozone is growing."[2] The following classic Dr. Laura conversation perfectly illustrates that truth and how easily both family and close relationships are destroyed because of it.

> *Dr. Laura:* Hello M____, welcome to the program.
> *Caller:* Hello? How are you doing?
> *Dr. Laura:* Hi, what can I do for ya?
> *Caller:* Well, I have a problem. I have this really great girl but uh . . . for the past six months I've been cheating on her . . . and I kinda want to tell her . . .
> *Dr. Laura:* Uh huh.
> *Caller:* . . . and I think the biggest problem is that I've been cheating with her sister.

Dr. Laura: Uh-hmmm.

Caller: And . . . I mean I . . . I really like her, but I don't know if I'm just . . . if I'm just a pig or if I can't help myself or . . .

Dr. Laura: You're a pig.

Time out for a minute. If it seems a bit uncharitable or irreligious to call someone a pig, please note that Dr. Laura is simply agreeing with the caller's own assessment—not that she needs any help in the blunt department!

Caller: . . . or well—

Dr. Laura: You're a pig! You can help yourself. You and her sister are *both* pigs!

Caller: OK . . . so . . . I mean, what . . . what should I do from this point on?

Dr. Laura: Not see either one of them anymore . . . and get some spiritual assistance.

Caller: You see, but the . . . the problem is that, you know I—

Dr. Laura: No, there's no problem other than you should see neither one of them anymore because that would destroy their family—*and* you should get some spiritual assistance!

Caller: OK . . . see, the point is that I actually have talked to a priest before.

Dr. Laura: Well that's very good, but it didn't work.

Caller: Yeah, that's why I figured . . .

Dr. Laura: Nothing worked. The priest cannot force you to be a man of character.

Caller: Yeah, I know . . . I understand that.

Dr. Laura: Priests can only define what a man of character is, and then you have to act . . . what you are doing now is very destructive to both women and their family. You should stop if you care at all about either one of them. You should stop seeing either one of them ever again.

Caller: See, that's the problem. I really like both of them—

Dr. Laura: No, you don't. You don't care about anyone but yourself. You are hurting both of them and their family and you don't care about that as long as your needs are satisfied. That is a pig.

Caller: [At this point, the caller simply, and ironically, only grunts, "Mmphh!"]

Dr. Laura: . . . and I appreciate your call (I think!).

Self-centeredness, about 99.999 percent of the time (I did the math), is what causes the problems that threaten the stability of our relationships. Many other types of problems may assail us, but if we are selfless, loving people, they can be dealt with. Ego, however, is not so easily dispatched. What was it that someone said about "a man wrapped up in himself makes a pretty small package"?

True character is not manifested in knowing right from wrong—though it begins there. True character manifests itself in actively rejecting what is wrong and doing what you believe is right. Whether you like it or not. Whether you want to or not. Whether it serves your needs or not. Whether it helps you or not. The single biggest obstacle to virtuous character is numero uno. Self-centeredness and good character are, from a biblical point of view, mutually exclusive. So what's going on here?

Sin 101 . . . Back to Eden's Drawing Board

Take the very first sin for example (remember the fruit thing?). God was clear, and both Adam and Eve knew what was allowed and what wasn't. It was what they chose to do in spite of what they knew that demonstrated a weakness of character.

Eden teaches us that the root of every act of wrong doing is selfishness. Catering to our own personal lusts. Self-gratification. What my grandmother used to call the "give me-have you got-and I want" mentality.

In 1 John 2:16, we find described the temptations Eve faced.

Namely, "the lust of the flesh, the lust of the eyes, and the pride of life" (KJV). That's why Eve ignored God. She centered on herself.

"When the woman saw that the tree was good for eating" (*My, that looks tasty*—lust of the flesh), and a "delight to the eyes" (*Oh, that's so beautiful*—lust of the eyes), and that the "tree was desirable to make one wise" (*Imagine how smart I'll become*—pride of life), she took of its fruit and ate." And so did her husband!

The caller and his first girlfriend were having sex outside of marriage. Why? Lust of the flesh. It felt good, so they did it. Then the guy became attracted to his girlfriend's sister. Why? Lust of the eyes. Then they started sleeping around behind the other sister's back! Now his ego is growing. Why? Pride of life. Both sisters have fallen for him.

When speaking with Craig Hamilton in an interview for *What Is Enlightenment* magazine, Dr. Laura spoke briefly of the "abdication of character" and, in the process, explained the "Mr. and Mrs. Pig" in all of us.

> We've all gone back to idol worship, and you know what the idol is? Where's my mirror? Me! That's our idol worship. Really! We walk around with mirrors. What pleases "me"? What will make "me" look good? What will make "me" feel good? Me. *Me!* If you have everybody doing that, if you and I are doing that, then I'm not caring about you and you're not caring about me (except for what we might get from each other), and we'll both be empty and hungry and lonely. The abdication is of values and ideals.[3]

When we stop to think about it, we could say that the main consequence of self-centered wrongdoing seems to be division. Everywhere you look people are at odds with other people. Half of our nation's marriages are ending in divorce, with the accompanying half of the nation's children being shattered by it. We have neighbor against neighbor. Race against race. Labor unions against companies and vice versa. People attacking each other, verbally and physically, on DPTV (Despicable People's TV). All for lack of decency. All for lack of character. All because we have rebelled against our Creator. We haven't yet learned that, in militating against God, we militate against ourselves individually, filially, and societally.

This is all fueled by lack of character, which stems from our rebelling against God and His directions for life. Virtuous character is neither born nor cultivated in a moral vacuum. It is determined by learning what's right, believing in what's right, and practicing what we know to be right. Adherence to biblical ethics will produce the selfless morality that makes a life better, a society better, a whole nation better—one person, one family, and one community which takes them to heart at a time.

Courage—Character of Heroic Proportions

Courage is not the absence of fear; it is the presence of character. True heroes are not those who are unafraid but those who are able to do what is right—even when they are afraid, no matter how great the self-sacrifice.

The right thing—especially and increasingly in our society—is seldom the easy thing to do. In fact, the degree of difficulty in doing the right thing is usually in direct proportion to the amount of virtue involved! Dr. Laura has a rather simple formula for this.

> There is a very easy way to figure out what the right thing to do is. Ask yourself, "Is this gonna be hard? Is this gonna be uncomfortable or even painful for me? Is it going to cost me something?" If you can answer yes to any or all of these, then there's your answer. *That* will usually be the right thing to do. The wrong thing is usually the easiest thing to do.

It is so much easier to put self ahead of God and others. In the following conversation, we see very clearly how tempting it can be for all of us to take the easy way out.

Dr. Laura: K_____, welcome to the program!

40

Caller: Hi, Dr. Laura! My problem is my brother, who is forty, and my two sons, who are sixteen and twelve. In a few days, he will be flying in for the holidays, and my brother's girlfriend will be coming with him.

Dr. Laura: Uh-hmmm.

Caller: I'm just wondering . . . although we haven't broached the subject yet, I'm not very comfortable with letting them sleep in the same bedroom.

Dr. Laura: You've never heard this show before?

Caller: Yes, I have.

Dr. Laura: Have you ever heard me deal with this subject before?

Caller: Yes.

Dr. Laura: And what have you heard me say?

Caller: Well, it's my home, and I should do as I want . . . and since I feel uncomfortable with it, I should take a stand and say so.

Dr. Laura: OK . . . now, what different direction would you like me to take? Since you already know where I'd go with that, what would be new here?

Caller: Nothing's new. I guess . . . you know, before I had my two children, it wouldn't have been a big deal—

Dr. Laura: Whoa, whoa, whoa—wait a minute! You already know the answer! If you don't have the guts to do it, then go ahead and let this go on in your home. Be weak so that your children will know you are weak. And then they will learn something about what they can get away with, all because Mommy doesn't want to "cause a problem."

Caller: Mmmphh . . . well . . .

Dr. Laura: And so it goes. What do you think? That there is a right answer for everybody else, but we have a way around it for you?

Caller: Well, no . . . I . . .

Dr. Laura: Well then, honest to gosh. Since you knew the answer [lowers voice to a whisper], why did you make the phone call?

Caller: I guess I just . . . I wanted to hear it out loud.

Dr. Laura: But you heard it out loud in other calls—you told me that. There's nothing different for you. There is an answer for what is right and what is wrong. Right only triumphs when people have the courage to stand by it. Courage is very important to goodness.

Caller: This is true.

Dr. Laura: Goodness requires courage. So, way before he comes, you call him up and say, "Here's the deal. I have children. Sleeping together out of wedlock is not the value system in my house. I am not telling you what to do; I am just telling you what's going to happen in my house. You guys either stay in separate rooms or stay at this local, little, adorable place I found.

Caller: OK. That's what I was planning on doing, and then I kinda wavered and . . .

Dr. Laura: And what made you waver?

Caller: I don't know, I thought if I . . . if I didn't make a big deal out of it, then my children probably wouldn't notice anyway, and it would just . . .

Dr. Laura: Really!

Caller: . . . be more of a burden to me . . .

Dr. Laura: They wouldn't notice? What is there around the house that you do or say or that comes in or out of it that they don't notice?

Caller: Well, that's true. I guess I was just *hoping* that they wouldn't notice.

Dr. Laura: As I said, cowardice is the only thing that lets goodness get overtaken by badness.

Caller: True, true . . . well, I think I need to call him and just make it clear . . .

Dr. Laura: Yeah!

Caller: . . . and if they have a problem with it, well then, there are plenty of motels around.

Dr. Laura: And that is what they will probably do.

Caller: Well, then that will save me a lot of grief [relieved laughter].
Dr. Laura: There ya go!
Caller: Well, thank you very much!
Dr. Laura: All right, honey, bye-bye.
Caller: Bye-bye, you have a nice day.
Dr. Laura: You too.

That's one thing I really appreciate about Mother Laura. She refuses to let people wiggle off the hook! Look at what was at stake with this caller:

- Was she or wasn't she going to be courageous about her own personal conviction? Was she going to be true to herself by taking a firm and unequivocal stand for what she believed was right? When you voluntarily unbar the gate, you surrender the whole fort.
- Was she or wasn't she going to teach her children that you have to stick by your principles by refusing to condone shacking up under her own roof?
- Was she or wasn't she going to model moral courage for both her children and her brother by showing them that people cannot go against their conscience or tolerate wrongdoing just to avoid unpleasant confrontations?

Bottom line is, was she going to teach her children to do what was right even if it wasn't easy? The key statement she made was this: "I thought if I . . . if I didn't make a big deal out of it, then my children probably wouldn't notice anyway, *and it would just be more of a burden to me.*" That has to be the least exclusive club on earth. The temptation to give in to evil because it's a burden to stand against it. The lack of courage, then, has the same taproot as lack of character: preoccupation with self.

We can all make a profound difference in both the quality of our own lives and our national character by refusing to back down from what's right. But we must begin with ourselves. With our own struggles and decisions. With our own family issues. Then we don't back down in our neighborhoods and in our schools. We don't back down at our churches, at town meetings, and at the ballot box. We call good, *good*; evil, *evil*; and practice what we preach.

Conscience: The Inner Law of Right and Wrong

The *American Heritage Dictionary* defines *conscience* as "the awareness of a moral or ethical aspect to one's conduct together with the urge to prefer right over wrong . . . conformity to one's own sense of right conduct."[4] Irving Layton, the Canadian poet, defined it in simpler terms: conscience is "self-esteem with a halo." I like that too, though it speaks more to the end result of having a good conscience.

When we know that we have done the right thing, we can take pride in that. We can feel good about ourselves. Although the role of self-esteem in character development is grossly overrated (one of Dr. Laura's pet peeves), everyone agrees that two benefits of a clear conscience are self-respect and dignity. The best way to obtain respect for yourself is to earn it. When you have confronted a moral dilemma and courageously done the right thing, your conscience will be the first to let you know.

The following example illustrates the power of conscience.

Dr. Laura received a copy of a letter written to a congressman by a Vietnam veteran. While this soldier was serving, it came to his attention that forty-five men were pinned down in a firefight and were about to be overrun by the enemy. The only way to rescue them was to send some choppers in through airspace that was officially off-limits. So he faced a moral dilemma. He could follow his orders (and put his military career in jeopardy) or he could save the lives of forty-five men. He ordered the choppers in. Later, the commanding general reviewed the reports and met privately with the soldier. He looked him in the eye and asked, "If you had to do all this over again, would you do it the same way?" This brave and noble soldier returned the general's gaze and replied, "Yes sir!"

What was so moving about all of this, Dr. Laura contended, was that none of the men ever knew that their lives were saved from sure death because some selfless person thought enough of them to disobey orders. "This," declared a deeply moved Dr. Laura, "is an honorable man."

Figuratively speaking, conscience is our moral "highway patrol." With its moral sensitivity radar, it monitors how we're driving down the highway of life. If we speed here, make an illegal U-turn there, or go the wrong way down a one-way street, it's going to pull us over with lights and sirens blazing and lecture us about the violation we've committed. We may grouse about it and mutter under our breath in protest, but in our bones most of us know we are guilty as charged, that is—guilty as we charge ourselves.

From the biblical perspective, our conscience—to a point—refers us to God's standards. In Romans 2:12-15, the Apostle Paul explains that just as Jews were held accountable to follow the Law of Moses, so Gentiles were held accountable to follow the law of their conscience.

> All who sin apart from the law will also perish apart from the law, and all who sin under the law will be judged by the law. For it is not those who hear the law who are righteous in God's sight, but it is those who obey the law who will be declared righteous. (Indeed, when Gentiles, who do not have the law, do by nature things required by the law, they are a law for themselves, even though they do not have the law, since they show that the requirements of the law are written on their hearts, their consciences also bearing witness, and their thoughts now accusing, now even defending them.)

You see, there are what we could call fundamental, moral laws of God. In every age and culture, humankind has generally known that it is wrong to murder, steal, lie, inflict violence on another, etc. Some things have always been and will always be wrong. For the most part, because we are made in the image of God, we know what they are. So our consciences are fairly accurate gauges by which we and God can assess the kind of people we really are.

> ### "I'm Not Proud of What I Did"

Dr. Laura considered the following conversation to be so significant that she made it her "call of the month" in the second edition of her *Go Take on the Day* newsletter. It illustrates, in a practical way, how the conscience of a young woman pressured her to "get back on track."

> *Caller:* Dr. Laura, I made a conscious choice to make a stupid decision. It's been about four years since I've been in a relationship. I've dated, but I went only so far after dating so many times, and then I moved on. If the relationship wasn't productive or healthy or just went other directions . . . anyway, I met a man and immediately felt too comfortable with him—extremely recently—and made the decision immediately to, in the afternoon, instead of continuing to watch the football game, not to watch the football game, and I . . .
>
> *Dr. Laura:* Decided to score in a different way?
>
> *Caller:* I slept with him, and . . . I am disappointed in myself, and I am not . . . I'm not proud of what I did. And yet, he is someone that I wish I could still get to know. However, if you show a certain character up front, you can't go back and say "that's not who I am."
>
> *Dr. Laura:* Wait, wait, wait, wow, wow, wow. Wow, wow, wow, wow [you can always tell when Dr. Laura is impressed with someone]. You are feeling uncomfortable and saying, "I did this and you know, this doesn't fit well with me; this is not how I am wanting to be. Therefore, I am backing off from that behavior." *That is* what character is about. It's about assessing our actions and acknowledging sometimes that we're off our own track. *That's what guilt is all about; it's about a message from inside that we are off our own track.* So when you get off your own track, you get

back on it. That is character!

Caller: Can you get back on it and continue to see if the other person also feels the same?

Dr. Laura: I don't know . . . if he just wants to put-it-to-you-baby; then, no.

Caller: I don't feel that way, no.

Dr. Laura: I have no idea what he's like.

Caller: Right.

Dr. Laura: So, you can't ask me the question, "If I get back on track, will he be on the same track?" The reason for getting back on track is that you are truer to yourself and don't feel disappointed and lacking in pride.

Caller: Right.

Dr. Laura: If he's not interested in a woman on that track, then it's not a match.

Caller: I guess I almost want to "cut and run" because I'm embarrassed.

Dr. Laura: I . . . well . . . see now, that's not character.

Caller: Right.

Dr. Laura: Then you would be disappointed and not proud of yourself again. And I don't know why, but I have this feeling that you do cut and run a lot.

Caller: I have before, in the past.

Dr. Laura: Yes, well, let's change that. Let's face it. Let's just tell him, "I got way off-track for what's right for me. I really like you. I really would like to get to know you. You really look great to me in so many ways, but of course I don't know you very well, but I just feel very comfortable, I just feel some kind of affinity. But this kind of behavior was inappropriate for me."

Caller: Saying that then would make me very proud of myself, regardless of the outcome.

Dr. Laura: Yes! That's the whole point. That is character! An experiment that didn't work is not a lack of character unless it is continuous.

Caller: No . . . that's right!

Dr. Laura: You see, that character has a lifelong timeline to it.

Caller: OK. I think to follow through with what you just said is much more important to me than the outcome of this one [relationship].

Dr. Laura: What you just said is a very spiritual understanding. That the point to your life is not his acceptance, but it is the quality of your behavior.

Caller: And being proud, looking in the mirror and being proud of what and how I follow through on this.

Dr. Laura: That's very spiritual; I'm terribly impressed!

Caller: Thank you for being there; you've helped me. Thank you for being there for all of us. It means a lot to me to listen to you on a regular basis, because you've helped me tremendously.

Dr. Laura: Thank you. Take care.

I was so impressed that I remember the call too. Here was a woman who did something wrong. More than shallow, more than superficial—it was immoral. But because a "requirement" of the law of God was written on her heart, her conscience "accused her." She knew the difference between right and wrong. At that point, she was forced to acknowledge to herself that she was "guilty" of wrongdoing. What she was wrestling with was how to make a course correction and get back on the track she knew she should be on. That is exactly how our consciences are supposed to work.

If every single individual currently shacking up, sleeping around for casual recreation, or pursuing a mutually destructive relationship could summon the courage to follow what is morally upright, the quality of our lives would improve dramatically. Granted, that might depend on what the meaning of the word *quality* is (for those who prefer their morality "relative"). But I really do think that preventing unwanted pregnancies would be good. Eliminating venereal diseases would be good. Dropping relationships that will never go anywhere because of a lack of commitment and maturity, or because the people involved have nothing of substance to offer one another, would be good. For those who believe quality equals self-gratification, then your conscience will not be morally sensitive enough to help you anyway.

Arteriosclerosis of the Soul

I do believe the biggest hobgoblin of conscience today is moral insensitivity. There is a rare affliction called congenital insensitivity to pain. It is a hereditary condition and is frequently fatal. What is it exactly? Every once in a great while we hear of a child in a Third World country who cannot feel any kind of pain. If he falls down and breaks a leg, he doesn't feel it—he only knows there is something wrong because he walks funny. And if he takes a serious fall down a rocky slope, he is apt to go home—and die. He didn't know he was bleeding internally. That's why people with that condition rarely live long. Pain, as much as we dislike it, serves a vital purpose. It lets us know when something is wrong and signals us to take appropriate measures.

God has blessed us with a moral sensitivity so we "feel pained" by certain behaviors. Just as surely as a sprained ankle will keep us from putting too much weight on it, so a sore conscience keeps us from putting injurious burdens on our heart. Unfortunately, we live in a society that is developing a congenital insensitivity to guilt. We are constantly being told that right is wrong and wrong is right. We have been "morally rubbed" the wrong way so much that we have calluses on our consciences. We have become impervious to shame. Dr. Laura has observed numerous times that we have forgotten how to blush.

For example, we are so bombarded with images and scenarios of "implicitly sanctioned" casual sex (via all kinds of media), that we accept and practice that behavior without so much as a pinprick from our conscience. Scantily clad, near-nude images of men and women parade across the TV screen and billboard ads with such frequency that we (society) think that two silver dollars and a G-string is modest attire. Lying, cheating, and stealing have become so endemic to corporate success that they're viewed as a necessity. And where, pray tell, is the embarrassment, the remorse, the blushing, for any of this (or other) wrongdoing?

With repeated exposure to what initially pained a soft and sensitive conscience, we have become, to use the biblical phrase, hardened in heart. Jesus once said that hardness of heart among the men of His day allowed them to act treacherously against the wives of their youth through casual divorce. The phrase "hearts were hard" in Matthew 19:8 is an interesting one. The Greek word for it is *sklerokardia*. Looks familiar, doesn't it? Jesus was describing *arteriosclerosis* of the heart or soul. Whenever we do what is wrong without guilt, shame, or remorse, we, too, show exactly how hardened our hearts have become. We defeat the purpose of having a conscience.

No One Said It Would Be Easy

"The basic premise of my radio program and books has been that, regardless of emotional angst or tremendous temptation . . . to benefit maximally from life, you must get back to the three C's: character, courage, and conscience."[5] Dr. Laura is *forever* pointing out that her admonitions toward goodness are exceedingly pragmatic—or maximally beneficial, as she puts it. She is quite correct. Virtue is not "theoretically" helpful; it *is* helpful. She is also correct to point out that we must rise to the occasion regardless of how difficult it is.

Too many of Dr. Laura's callers (like all of us), try to excuse poor decisions and bad behaviors by saying that the temptation was just too difficult to resist. People rationalize their moral surrender with phrases like, "Well, I just can't help myself!" "It's just too hard!" "You don't know what I'm going through!" or "You don't know what I've been through!" But Dr. Laura never lets them get away with it. One of her classic responses to caller rationales is to say, "Hey, no one put a gun to your head, you *chose* to do that!" Invariably the response is, "You're right . . . you're absolutely right." They (we) simply give in to pressure too easily.

I remember the time Dr. Laura asked her listeners to fax in

their official lists of "Ten Darn Good Reasons Not to Bother Being Moral." Guess what was cited as the number one reason *not* to be moral—*it was easier!* Surprise, surprise! If we would aspire to being truly brave people, then we must put what is right ahead of what is easy.

"All right then," Dr. Laura began one segment,

> Here is a cover story in *USA Today*. It is disheartening. At one point it gets really annoying and aggravating. So I want to bring it to your attention. It says, "Nearly half of United States people who have jobs admit to taking unethical or illegal actions in the past year." Now mind you, this is probably an underestimation, and I'll tell you why. If half the workers interviewed admitted it, you've got to know that a lot of them lied that they didn't. So the number is probably higher. Two, they only ask people to list violations that they attributed to pressure. This is where I got angry. Let me read you a little bit of this. It says, "These include one or more from a list of twenty-five actions, including cheating on an expense account, discriminating against coworkers, paying or accepting kickbacks, secretly forging signatures, trading sex for sales, and looking the other way when environmental laws are violated. The 236-page report is especially sobering because workers were asked only to list violations that they attributed to pressure. Due to long hours, sales quotas, job insecurity, balancing work and family, and personal debt for example. It didn't ask about unethical or illegal actions for other reasons—such as greed, revenge, and blind ambition."
>
> So that's another reason it is bigger. This story goes on and you actually find some people almost apologizing for their behavior because of pressure.
>
> First of all, the reason that these people do these unethical things is not pressure. That's a lie. That's an absolute lie. Falsehood. The reason people do unethical and

illegal things is because they don't have a value system. The whole point of having a value system is to help you withstand pressure. If there's no pressure, what the heck do you need values for, right?

This is just awful. "Most ethics experts agree that job pressure is the leading cause of unethical behavior by workers." Well, most ethics experts are morons, if that's their conclusion, because it's wrong. It isn't because of pressure. It's because of a lack of values, period.

For the Christian, the personification of values is Jesus Christ. No one ever resisted pressure for the sake of doing what was right more successfully than He. There was too much riding on it for you and me. The following story is one of many examples we could use from His life.

"If you are the Son of God, tell these stones to become bread," so ordered the Adversary (Matthew 4:3). When you haven't eaten for forty days, and you have the ability to make your own food—*that's pressure!* But not merely because your stomach is sticking to your backbone. This wasn't just about hunger. Jesus was lying at death's door. But He showed that the will of His Father was more important than His own. "It is written," He told the Enemy,

> Man does not live on bread alone, but on every word
> that comes from the mouth of God. (v. 4)

Spiritual life, He shows us, is more important than physical life. Trusting in God is more important than trusting in yourself. Had Jesus put Himself first, He would have been no different from anybody else. He would no longer have been our atoning "lamb without spot or blemish." He would have lost His moral authority as the Son of God. And He could not have been poured out as the perfect sacrifice. But He was willing to die before He would violate that trust.

What was it that Dr. Laura said? Why do you need values if you're under no pressure? It's no big deal to forgo food if you've just had a large, satisfying meal. But when the food means life and you forgo it for a principle . . . that's character, courage, and conscience.

"Just Can't Beat It" "Character, courage, and conscience" is not just Dr. Laura's mantra; it is a mantra of the Judeo-Christian Scriptures. True character gives birth to courage. Courage in choosing right over wrong gives birth to a clear conscience. Our clear conscience gives birth to self-respect, which reinforces the desire to keep our characters strong, clean, and good.

Perhaps all of this has been said best by an old Southern gentleman (as quoted in *Christianity* magazine): "Ya just can't beat doin' right. I ain't seen nothin' in all my life that'd beat it!"

Dr. Laura couldn't agree more. That is precisely why, when she says, "I think you are doing the right thing," she adds, "That's one of the nicest things I can say to any person."

Of Motherhood and God

It isn't news to my longtime listeners and those who read my books that I've undergone profound changes over the course of my life—the most important of which is my journey from basic atheist to observant Jew. In my twenties, I was my own moral authority . . . the inadequacy of that way of life is painfully obvious today. At the same time, my early experiences have taught me how much better it is to live by an objective and absolute standard of right and wrong, preferably, a standard set by God. That is the hard-won wisdom I try to pass along to others as I preach, teach, and nag every day on this program.

Dr. Laura

Losing God, Losing Ourselves

Despite what the polls say about our nation being a nation of "believers" in God, the people we read about in the papers, hear about in the news, work with, and meet in the street tell a different story. As I indicated in the introduction, there is a difference between mere intellectual assent and a deep-seated conviction that guides how we live our lives. True believers are constrained by their faith to think, talk, and act in ways that harmonize with the will of God. Bottom line, we either follow Him or we follow ourselves. The trouble with a faith that's only bumper-sticker deep is that when you become your own god, you are never going to be able to rise above yourself.

When our actions exclude God, no matter what "religious" words we use, nothing and no one else matters—just our opinions, our thoughts, our feelings. And that, as Dr. Laura observes, makes for a dangerous world.

Do you really believe that there's no set of values more important than the one you want for yourself? That's an interesting life. I for one find that scary, because some people think it's OK to loot and burn, do terrorism, and kill for their idea, for their feelings. I just heard something incredible when I was driving in. I scan through all the channels and listen to people, because you never know when you're going to learn something useful. Not that most of talk radio has information, but some of it does. In this one particular program they were talking to somebody who has followed the LAPD in South Central and the homicide squad. Really interesting information, I thought. Did you know that out of—what was it—fifty-five, fifty-nine, almost sixty people who were killed in the LA riots that not one person has been convicted of murder? I don't think this city would dare. Somehow that's OK. And this particular talk show host said he did a public venue where they showed a movie called *Riot* and talked to the people in the community about their *feelings* about it. And when he brought up that point, (that no one had prosecuted the rioters who committed all those crimes, including murder) they got angry with him. Why, there were "strong feelings!"

OK. Well, if people can make up their own value system because they have strong feelings, and they're allowed to murder, then you can see my point when there's nothing above that. Then your feelings become your god. Your guiding light. Think about it. I know that selfishly, we each want the freedom to do whatever the heck we want to do; but pragmatically, does a family work that way? Does a people really work that way?

Of course not. Society doesn't work well at all that way, though it's not for lack of trying. There is a New Testament passage that cites an extensive litany of consequences that accompany "losing God." As you read these verses, see if they don't remind you of the way things are nowadays.

For since the creation of the world God's invisible qualities—his eternal power and divine nature—have been clearly seen, being understood from what has been made, so that men are without excuse. For although they knew God, they neither glorified him as God nor gave thanks to him, but their thinking became futile and their foolish hearts were darkened. Although they claimed to be wise, they became fools and exchanged the glory of the immortal God for images made to look like mortal man and birds and animals and reptiles.

Therefore God gave them over in the sinful desires of their hearts to sexual impurity for the degrading of their bodies with one another. They exchanged the truth of God for a lie, and worshiped and served created things rather than the Creator—who is forever praised. . . .

Furthermore, since they did not think it worthwhile to retain the knowledge of God, he gave them over to a depraved mind, to do what ought not to be done. They have become filled with every kind of wickedness, evil, greed and depravity. They are full of envy, murder, strife, deceit and malice. They are gossips, slanderers, God-haters, insolent, arrogant and boastful; they invent ways of doing evil; they disobey their parents; they are senseless, faithless, heartless, ruthless. Although they know God's righteous decree that those who do such things deserve death, they not only continue to do these very things but also approve of those who practice them. (Romans 1:20-25, 28-32)

That could have been written in today's paper about our own society. Evil flourishes where faith in God does not.

No God, No Purpose

So, just how *did* Dr. Laura, an atheist, come to faith as an Orthodox Jew? I found out recently while listening to a speech she gave in

Ottawa, Canada, in May 1998. Here is how her speech began:

> I want! I want! (I don't want, my mother gives me every-
> thing.) But I want. I want to *want*. We don't know why
> or what . . . but we want.
>
> But what is life really all about? What does it all
> mean? Why am I here? What really matters?

She then began to talk about all the things throughout her life
that she just knew would bring her happiness. First, she wanted to be
thin. While she's always been a "micro-person," there were, nonetheless, other girls in high school who were thinner than she was. So, eat
less. Get thinner. Be happy. Now this was what life was about!

Next she wanted smarts. Get good grades. Be a studyaholic.
There she would find meaning. There she would find purpose.
There she would find happiness.

Then came the subject of God. "We had discussions in college
about God, and I felt as though this topic was like the Twilight Zone—
a burning bush that doesn't burn? Get real! How could any educated,
thinking person find meaning in that?" she thought at the time.

Then love! Ah . . . find a cute guy to spend your life with . . .
that's the ticket!

Next, Dr. Laura immersed herself in the pursuit of a career. Far
be it from her to betray the "sisterhood" and put herself under the
thumb of the same patriarchal system that had oppressed women
since the beginning of time. No way was she going to become *just* a
wife and mother. She was woman . . . time to roar, baby!

Please do not misunderstand what Dr. Laura was trying to say
here. There is nothing wrong with any of the above "wants." Taking
care of your health and appearance is a good thing. Likewise, aca-
demic excellence and a successful career are worthy objectives. All of
them are accomplishments that are a part of a well-lived life, and
they *contribute* to our happiness. But if we are going to pursue them
from a strictly materialistic point of view as if they're pots of gold at
the end of the rainbow, we will find true fulfillment and purpose no
less elusive.

As Dr. Laura continued her speech, she spoke of the years she labored under the impression that, "If *I* look good, if *I* perform satisfactorily, if *I* find someone, if *I* am successful, then *I'll* find happiness."

Her statement had such a familiar ring to it that I thought, "Now where have I heard that before?"

Then I remembered the fellow that also suffered from a severe case of *"I"* strain. Jesus once told the parable of a wealthy man whose crops came in even more abundantly than usual. His musings sounded remarkably like Dr. Laura's:

"He thought to himself, 'What shall *I* do? I have no place to store *my* crops.' Then he said, 'This is what *I'll* do. I will tear down my barns and build bigger ones, and there *I* will store all *my* grain and *my* goods. And *I'll* say to *myself,* 'You have plenty of good things laid up for many years. Take life easy; eat, drink, and be merry." (Luke 12:17-19 emphasis added)

Unfortunately for the foolish rich man, God demanded his life that very night. "Then who will get what you have prepared for yourself?" God asks him. Jesus drives His point home by saying, "This is how it will be with anyone who stores up things for himself but is not rich toward God."

Poor fellow. What do you suppose he thought about in the final hours of his life? I strongly suspect that he asked himself the same question Dr. Laura did: *"Is this all there is?"*

Finding God, Finding Purpose

Dr. Laura began to find the answer to her question when she and her husband Lew were watching a PBS special on reproduction. As a college professor who had taught physiology at the University of Southern California, she already knew the processes at work—it was old hat. Nevertheless, she found herself crying at the end of the hour when the newborn was laid upon the mother's bosom while the new father watched. Lew looked over at Laura and knowingly said, "I think you want to become a mother."

The pivotal moment came a couple of years later when Deryk was born. When the tiny miracle whom she had given a long and arduous birth to brushed his chubby cheek against her, and suckled at her breast, it was as if God whispered, *Hello, Laura . . . welcome to the program.*

Through that tiny miracle came another—a dawning awareness of God. There must be a God . . . just had to be. This little precious human being was too perfect, too amazing, to be an accident.

At the same time Laura began to realize she needed to be living for something, for someone, outside of herself. It was the beginning of a journey that led her to true joy and meaning. As she gazed at her newborn son, the *I* was replaced by *You.*

This "awareness of God" and the discovery of purpose is something we need to take a closer look at.

Life from Life Suggests God

As I continued listening to Dr. Laura's Ottawa speech, I couldn't help but be reminded how scriptural all of her main points were. She had taught about life's biology, physiology, and chemistry, but it wasn't until she looked at the child she and her husband made *and* became intimately connected to, that she perceived something wondrous. She saw the handiwork of God and realized, finally, that He must be! As she spent those first few hours with her baby, Romans 1:20 literally came to life for her.

> *For since the creation of the world God's invisible qualities—
> his eternal power and divine nature—have been clearly seen,
> being understood from what has been made. . . .*

As a minister, I often talk with people who have doubts about the existence of God. For me, Romans 1:20 is a natural starting point because the most obvious implication of life . . . is *life*. Life *always* comes from life, from a Lifegiver.

A good friend of mine, Rodger Trimm, who preaches for the Church of Christ in El Centro, California, wrote a lovely piece of verse that expresses this beautiful and obvious truth.

The Grinning Pup

I saw a grinning pup,
Running in the wind.
A grinning, speckled pup,
Running with a friend.
The boy, not far behind,
Laughed for all his worth.
The two were joined in mind,
By love, and love of mirth.
Where did it all begin, this homo-canis bond?
In evolution's bin? Or did a God so fond,
Of elemental joy,
Create a grinning pup?
Create a laughing boy?
I know what I believe.

For those raised with faith, faith in God typically comes first through the revelation of Himself in His Word and as explained by their parents. But for many like Dr. Laura, who were raised without that kind of instruction, they come to believe in God through the revelation of nature. They just needed to "be still, and know that I am God" (Psalm 46:10).

Dr. Laura asked the question in her speech, "Are we just accidents of egg and sperm? Are we a random assembling of molecules that just happen to get together by chance?" She answered the question with a story:

> This scientific-minded fellow was "waxing eloquent" to a rabbi about how there is no reason to believe that anything in life has a master architect. We can take chemicals, water, building blocks of life, and with all we know—we just have to get a little bit smarter—soon we'll be able to create life. It's all chemistry, it's all physics, it's all math. No need to invoke God.
>
> The rabbi responded by handing the skeptic a beautiful, calligraphied poem on a piece of parchment. The

parchment was incredibly beautiful. The script was elegant. But the poem transcended both with its profound message, its deep insights, and its eloquent expression. The skeptic looked up after reading it and asked, with tears in his eyes, "Who wrote this?"

The rabbi answered, "Well, actually, no one wrote it. I had this beautiful piece of parchment laid out on my table and a bottle of ink up on the shelf. My cat, in jumping off the shelf down to the table, knocked the ink off, and it puddled up on the table next to the parchment. While my cat lay upon the table throughout the night, it swished its tail back and forth from ink puddle to parchment . . . well, you can see the result. That was all done when I woke up this morning."

Well, since you put it like that! Yes, it does seem sort of silly that something like creation could just happen. Yet popular thinking today believes in the "swishing tail" theory, and it's called evolution.

This is such an important point that I want to elaborate just a bit because if we are nothing more than a cosmic hiccup, then discussions about meaning and purpose are absurd.

I won't get into a discussion here about the differences between micro- and macroevolution. Suffice to say that science has documented certain evolutionary changes within species. I'm not talking about that. But science has not yet demonstrated that:

- Life can come from nonlife, that is, spontaneous generation
- One species can evolve into another completely different species

The key point, of course, is spontaneous generation. Did life begin in Campbell's Cream of Primordial? A little of this? A little of that? With just a pinch of whatever energy would have been necessary to get the process going? If it did, then God did not create humankind—humankind created Him out of our evolved imaginations.

The single biggest problem with the theory of evolution, however, is that it assumes—has to assume—that life came from nonlife. But all of our everyday observations, including scientific, are to the contrary. Life always comes from life. Every life form we've ever seen has come from life just like itself. No exceptions. Everything producing "according to [their] kind[s]" (Genesis 1). That's grasses, herbs, trees, flowers, insects, fish, reptiles, and mammals, etc., etc., etc. The biblical statement is not only in perfect harmony with what we see everyday, it is in perfect harmony with what science observes everyday!

In *The Lost World*, by Michael Crichton, the main characters discount creationism as "just plain wrong . . . God is not at work. No higher organization principle was involved. In the end, we are just the result of a bunch of mutations that either survives or dies."

Later, in that same novel, Crichton gives an honest and graphic illustration of the mathematical improbabilities associated with the genetic mutations or "accidents" required to bring about major evolutionary changes.

Imagine a tornado that cuts a large swath through this junkyard. It throws zillions of pieces of junk of all kinds, shapes, sizes, materials, etc., into the air, swirls them around violently, exerts incredible forces upon them, and leaves assembled in its wake a fully constructed and fully functional 747 airplane! "It's very hard to believe," says the main character of the book.

Yes! It is!

That is why people like Dr. Laura and myself contend that it is more reasonable to believe in God than not. Because design implies a designer. Mathematical combinations imply a mathematician. Chemistry implies a chemist. Physics imply a physicist. Engineering implies an engineer. *Life implies life!*

Why, then, do some people look at life and see it as a "random assembling of molecules"? Dr. Laura suggests that it allows us to avoid accountability to a Higher Being and a higher standard of conduct. It permits us to live for ourselves, according to our own value systems. Being dismissive about God, about a Heavenly Father, makes it very easy for us.

See what holding a newborn babe can do for some folks?

Life for Life Suggests God

A life lived in awareness of God also means a life lived in awareness of others. Loving, thoughtful parents who listen to God will realize how incompatible self-centeredness is with the role of being a mother and father. Dr. Laura certainly did. Her newborn son taught her a lot.

The next pivotal step in her journey toward God occurred a few years later, when she and young Deryk were watching a television program about the Holocaust. She relates the story in her book *The Ten Commandments: The Significance of God's Laws in Everyday Life*.

> One rainy Sunday, Deryk, then about six or seven, and I were channel-surfing. My finger froze on the remote turner when the visual image appeared on our TV screen of scores of naked women, holding their equally doomed babies, huddled along the ridge of a deep pit in the earth, waiting for the Nazi soldiers' bullets to end their fear. My son's mouth opened in amazed horror. . . .
>
> "Momma," Deryk screamed out, grabbing me, "what is happening?"
>
> "Honey," I tried to say calmly, "those are German soldiers in World War II, murdering mommies and their babies."
>
> "Momma, why are they doing that?"
>
> "They're evil."
>
> "Who are those women?"
>
> "The women and children are Jews."
>
> "Momma, who are Jews?"
>
> "Deryk, the Jews are our people. . . ."[1]

Our people. These women and children lived in another country, in another time. Dr. Laura and Deryk did not know them personally, and yet they were *our people*. Through empathy, compassion, and sorrow, they became more connected to these people—and to their own identity. This connection, and Deryk's questions about what a Jew is, led to Dr. Laura's study of Judaism and, ultimately, to her whole family's conversion.

If it is true, as Dr. Laura and I believe, that there is a God, One who created us and loves us, then everyone—no matter what color, race, or gender—is *our people*. And like Dr. Laura, if we embrace this truth it will have a profound impact on the way we live and relate to others.

That is why "Love the Lord your God with all your heart and with all your soul and with all your mind" is called the "first and greatest commandment. And the second is like it: 'Love your neighbor as yourself.' All the Law and the Prophets hang on these two commandments" (Matthew 22:37-40; Romans 13:8-10). If we base our regard for other people on our common heritage as image-bearers of God, then we are going to do the right thing by them. C.S. Lewis summed it up this way:

> It is a serious thing to live in a society of possible gods and goddesses, to remember that the dullest and most uninteresting person you talk to may one day be a creature which, if you saw it now, you would be strongly tempted to worship, or else a horror and a corruption such as you now meet, if at all, only in a nightmare. All day long we are, in some degree, helping each other to one or other of these destinations. It is in the light of these overwhelming possibilities, it is with the awe and the circumspection proper to them, that we should conduct all our dealings with one another, all friendships, all loves, all play, all politics. There are no *ordinary* people. You have never talked to a mere mortal. Nations, cultures, arts, civilizations—these are mortal, and their life is to ours as the life of a gnat. But it is immortals whom we joke with, work with, marry, snub, and exploit—immortal horrors or everlasting splendors.[2]

Dr. Laura is not the first to find God through creation and others. And she won't be the last. As a matter of fact, she's trying to show millions of people every day what this path is and how important it is. In the following conversation, which I was not able to listen to with dry eyes, I appreciated all the more how living for others is essential in making our lives meaningful.

> *Dr. Laura:* M_____, welcome to the program.
> *Caller:* Hi, Dr. Laura.
> *Dr. Laura:* Hi!
> *Caller:* I'm sixteen, and I'm bulimic or anorexic, whatever, both of them.
> *Dr. Laura:* Well, I don't know. What is it that you do? Without giving it a name, what is it that you do with food?
> *Caller:* Sometimes I starve myself, and then when I have to eat, I'll throw up.
> *Dr. Laura:* OK . . . so you do need medical intervention. What you're doing to yourself could kill you.
> *Caller:* The problem . . .
> *Dr. Laura:* You are aware of that, aren't you?
> *Caller:* Yeah, but I don't really care that it might kill me.
> *Dr. Laura:* Yes, but the "not caring" is temporary. Are there not some days you care more than other days?
> *Caller:* Sometimes.
> *Dr. Laura:* Aren't there some days you care a lot? Now be honest. Don't play dramatic on me. There are days you care a lot. You have good days in which you're blessed in your mind that you're alive.
> *Caller:* Yes.
> *Dr. Laura:* Right. And you have days you don't care.
> *Caller:* A lot of days I don't care.
> *Dr. Laura:* Right. I understand that. But part of why you don't care is how you choose to live your life.
> *Caller:* I guess so.
> *Dr. Laura:* Let me ask you one question. One very seri-

ous question. All right?

Caller: Uh huh.

Dr. Laura: What is it that you do that is strictly for somebody else's benefit?

Caller: Oh . . . I don't really understand what you're asking.

Dr. Laura: Well, do you volunteer time to deliver food to elderly people who can't get out of their homes?

Caller: No.

Dr. Laura: Do you go to the local orphanage and volunteer some time to play with the kids for about an hour and help them learn to color?

Caller: No.

Dr. Laura: Do you think people who do that see life as worthwhile?

Caller: Yeah.

Dr. Laura: You see . . . you're at that stage of life that people are very egocentric. Do you know what that means?

Caller: No.

Dr. Laura: Very focused in on yourself. How you feel at any moment. What somebody has said or done to you. All of this drama is generally taken very personally, and especially the negative part is taken personally. Because I could get you very easily to tell me fifteen ways you've been hurt this week by somebody. If I asked you for fifteen things that were pleasant, you'd struggle and not want to tell me.

Caller: Yeah.

Dr. Laura: Because you're picking out the negative . . .

Caller: OK.

Dr. Laura: And you know why?

Caller: Why?

Dr. Laura: Do you think—tell me the truth now, I want to see your vision about life—do you think it is strictly just a complete biological accident that you're here?

Caller: No.

Dr. Laura: Do you think there is any point to us being

here? Me? You? The people next door and people walking down the street?

Caller: I suppose so.

Dr. Laura: And what is everybody's purpose?

Caller: I have no idea.

Dr. Laura: Try. What is everybody's purpose?

Caller: I don't know.

Dr. Laura: Try. Try!

Caller: Everybody else has a different purpose.

Dr. Laura: Yeah. There is one general umbrella idea but we all do it individually. It's like when a team plays ball, the whole object is to win the game, but each has a different job to get them there. So as human beings, what is our team job?

Caller: To be happy.

Dr. Laura: No. And that's why you're miserable. Because you think the purpose of life is to be happy. And you get sad when something doesn't add to that. No. It isn't to be happy. As a matter of fact, when you pick that as a goal, you rarely, if ever, attain it. Happiness is a by-product of doing something meaningful. The only people I know who are truly, profoundly happy are those who do something constructive and see their lives as meaningful. Then they have a sense of personal satisfaction. A sense of purpose in life. Your job is to struggle to find what yours is. Not to focus on every piece of misery, everything your mom and dad said that you don't like, everything your friends did, how miserable you feel. Me, me, me, me. Because that'll make anyone get depressed. But when you get off the phone, I'd like you to sit there and think, "What can I do that somebody else will benefit from, because then I will automatically have purpose."

Caller: OK.

Dr. Laura: Your life has no purpose right now—but it can have. Your job is to find it. We are here to perfect the world. Your job, I don't know. You've got to find what your

68

position on the team is. And you can't do that by contemplating why you're not happy.

Caller: OK.

Dr. Laura: You've been given a blessed gift, an opportunity to help perfect the world. You have an opportunity to do something wonderful, and at sixteen, you're at the beginning of this journey. You have something important to do. I don't know what it is, and you may do a bunch of things before you find it. I know that was true for me.

Caller: Thank you.

Dr. Laura: OK, sweetheart?

Caller: Uh huh.

Dr. Laura: I want to hear about you one day.

Caller: OK.

Dr. Laura: I want somebody to say to me, you know, I met this lady M_____, and she did such and such, and it really touched my heart. OK?

Caller: Uh huh.

Dr. Laura: OK.

Caller: Thank you.

Dr. Laura: Thanks for your call.

Caller: Bye-bye.

What a wonderful and wonderfully edifying conversation that was! It's a good bet that this was the first time that young girl ever heard something so profound. Purpose comes through service to others. Meaning is derived from doing something outside of yourself. Joy and deep satisfaction are found in doing something good for somebody else. This is, after all, what we were made for.

That is why, for Christians, one of our greatest examples of what life is all about is found in what Jesus did in John 13:1-17, on the occasion of the Last Supper. Though He was about to be betrayed and crucified, He had one last, vitally important lesson to teach His disciples—the same disciples who were arguing with each other over who was going to be the "greatest" in the kingdom of God.

Jesus performed one of the most humble tasks imaginable in that day. He stooped down and washed His disciples' feet. Of course, they were taken aback. Peter actually said, "No, you shall never wash my feet!" He saw a huge contradiction in Jesus being Lord and doing such a menial chore.

But Jesus told Peter that he could have no part with Him unless He did wash his feet. He intended to teach Peter and the rest that it wasn't unlike their Lord to serve others at all. In fact, it was *just like Him* to do that! They needed to understand that serving the needs of others was precisely what He came to do; and if they were to be His followers, they would have to follow suit.

> Now that I, your Lord and Teacher, have washed your feet, you also should wash one another's feet. I have set you an example that you should do as I have done for you. I tell you the truth, no servant is greater than his master, nor is a messenger greater than the one who sent him. Now that you know these things, you will be blessed if you do them. (John 13:14-17)

A loss of awareness of or respect for God will result in a loss of respect for others—their rights, their property, their well-being, their very lives. That's why Dr. Laura has such a thriving "practice." Every single day she is called on to help solve a person's moral dilemma. Virtually without exception, that problem has been caused by ungodliness. Invariably, godliness—loving God and serving others—is the best solution.

So who needs to take control of our lives? Who is best equipped to help us *go take on the day?*

Dr. Laura suggests that God is. She frequently refers to many of the positive and dramatic changes that have come about in her life since she has come to believe in God. As one who used to call her own shots and direct her own steps, she knows what she is talking about. She knows what it is to look back on a morally "misspent youth" and feel pain and remorse for things she did as a young atheistic humanist. She once rolled her eyes when you mentioned God.

Now she believes in Him and lives for others. A sincere belief in God and the strong conviction that all of humankind is made in His image and is therefore sacred is what makes that possible for all of us.

The Need for Objective Standards

I have a moral health show . . . and it's not that *I'm* right, it's that *God* is right. I'm just reiterating the Ten Commandments. I dusted them off and am presenting them again. I'm not even interpreting them. Frankly, they don't need interpretation. They are so clear and so profound . . . they are the best blueprint we've ever had for a purposeful and meaningful life.

> *Dr. Laura's reaction to an assessment by a*
> *psychology professor who had written this about*
> *her: "A good psychotherapist helps people find their*
> *own answers. Basically, Dr. Laura is about, "I'm*
> *right, everybody else is wrong."'*

Dr. Laura contends that, since all authority resides with the Sovereign God, then His laws form the objective ethical standard to which we should adhere. They provide the blueprint we should use to construct the kind of blessed, joyful lives God intends for us to lead. Does this makes sense? Indeed it does.

Once you accept God as Creator, as the One whom the Bible depicts as the Heavenly Father, which is the more reasonable proposition: that a Father who lovingly created life in His image would leave that life to grope around blindly, only guessing as to what life is about and how it needs to be lived? Or that He would communicate to His creation much-needed principles and guidance? What would you do for your children?

The Need for Objective Standards

Merriam-Webster's Tenth Collegiate Dictionary defines *standard* this way:

> Something established by authority, custom, or general consent as a model or example: criterion; something set up and established by authority as a rule for the measure of quantity, weight, extent, value, or quality. [Synonyms are] *criterion, gauge, yardstick, touchstone.*

Our English word *standard* comes from the Old French *estandard*, which means "a rallying point." So, a standard is a place to rally, a place where one takes a stand—hard, fast, and unyielding. An ethical standard, then, would be the rallying point, the criterion or yardstick for what is right and wrong. Dr. Laura's program, since it became a moral health show based on the Ten Commandments, exhorts us to rally around God's standard, to measure our lives by His criterion.

Why do we need standards? Because of the benefits we derive from them. When we disregard standards, we also disregard their benefits. A standard is an all-or-nothing kind of thing. We can't "partially" use a standard. We can't "occasionally" use a standard when it suits us and discard it when it doesn't. Defeats the whole purpose. Let's step out of the ethical scene for a moment and think of what it would be like to get rid of standards in other areas. What kind of confusion do you suppose would ensue?

Say you go to the hardware store to buy a pound of tenpenny nails, twenty board feet of lumber, two square yards of tile, a quart of paint, a pint of turpentine, and order six cubic yards of concrete for the new patio. Don't you expect—even demand—that each respective measurement be exact and according to the common, objective standard? Not just to get what you pay for, but to avoid the massive mess that would result otherwise? Sure you do.

Whether we are talking about medication (500 milligrams, three times daily) or speed limits (55 miles per hour), then, we know that objective, universally observed standards are an absolute necessity in all areas of life. Without them—total chaos.

The following piece of research is not hypothetical but all too real. How mad does it make you?

> Bilking consumers out of pennies has now become a billion-dollar business. The *National Observer* noted that short weighing on food, gasoline, home fuel oil, packaged hardware items, and pills cost the American public some six to twelve billion dollars per year. In an effort to curb this swindle, whether accidental or intentional, many states are spot-checking weights and measures.
>
> Pennsylvania investigators discovered that 15.5 percent of all prepackaged foods checked were short-weighted, with some stores shorting on 25 percent of the packages checked. A three-day Kansas investigation turned up evidence that 30 percent of all meat packaged in eleven stores were short-weighted.
>
> In Arkansas, officials checked one-pound cans of vegetables to find none that contained sixteen ounces. And Tennessee officials found prepackaged pork chops short-weighted by up to thirty-one cents. Officials have tabulated forty-eight ways to cheat in weighing meat in front of customers, and many markets are apparently using some of them.[1]

There is a larger issue here, something more fundamentally important at stake. The real problem is not that we don't we have enough scales, weights, measures, bureaus, laws, rules, regulations, and lawyers. It's that the only real shortage of standards in this country are ethical ones. If more people adhered to those, we wouldn't need as many regulations—or lawyers.

This tells us something about the hierarchy of standards. We are trying to fix and control by regulation and litigation what would be better dealt with by inculcating simple honesty and integrity. When we remove God and His absolute authority from the picture, however, how are we going to do that? Secular, physical standards are important, but moral standards are so much more important.

How can we contend for the absolute indispensability of weights and measures, rules and regulations that govern how we deal with each other, and not see that God's objective ethical standards— and the morality they cultivate—are even more fundamental? How can we insist on the necessity of objective norms because of the chaos that would ensue without them *and not* insist on objective morality when we see how disastrous it's been for our society since we've abandoned it?

"Imperial Selves" as a Standard

It's not that people don't talk about values anymore. Everyone talks about values. But many times, it's our own values we talk about. We tend to measure ourselves by our own moral yardsticks and refuse to be judged by any other. This ethical relativism has become firmly entrenched as America's favorite philosophical norm, thanks largely to the '60s generation. It hardly originated with them, but they popularized it. The irony is, the generation that stood for "Peace, man" and "Make love, not war" promoted the very ethical relativism that makes true love and peace impossible.

An article in *U.S. News & World Report,* July 14, 1997, credited Fritz Perls for penning the motto of the Me Generation: "I do my thing, and you do your thing. I am not in this world to live up to your expectations, and you are not in this world to live up to mine."

That sounds so open-minded, doesn't it? So progressive. So liberating. So, so . . . self-centered. (Amazing how frequently that term keeps popping up in this book!) Dr. Laura summed it up this way, "I went to college in the late '60s . . . 'let it all hang out, baby . . . do what ya feel like . . . someone else has a problem with it, it's *their* problem.' Think about the egocentrism and the loss of any connection in these statements."

But the "best it's ever been said" award has to go to John Leo, a contributing editor for *U.S. News & World Report,* who appeared on Judith Regan's program to discuss certain aspects of America's deteriorating culture. He described the 1960s mind-set as "a nonaggression pact between imperial selves." Now that nails it, doesn't it! I'll leave you alone, and you leave me alone, because we are all our own authorities, accountable to no one.

The Achilles' heel of this self-serving philosophy, however, is seen in what happens when everyone around us starts thinking and acting as we do. When the shoe is on the other imperial self's foot, when what goes around comes around, we don't like it at all. Then we see the fallacy of our reasoning.

In one of my favorite "Calvin and Hobbes" cartoons, the little boy and his tiger are meandering through the woods, looking under rocks, jumping off logs, etc., while Calvin pontificates on ethics.

"I don't believe in ethics anymore. As far as I'm concerned, the ends justify the means. Get what you can while the getting's good—that's what *I* say! Might makes right! The winners write the history books! It's a dog-eat-dog world, so I'll do whatever I have to and let others argue about whether it's 'right' or not."

At this point, the wise Hobbes gives Calvin a sharp push from behind. Calvin's eyes bug out and he yells, "HEYY!" As he looks up from the gooey, brown mud that completely engulfs him, he shouts, "Why'd you do THAT?!?"

Hobbes says simply but with a smug smile, "You were in my way. Now you're not. The ends justify the means."

"I didn't mean for everyone, you dolt! Just me!"

"Ahh . . . ," says Hobbes as he walks away.[2]

The Judeo-Christian Scriptures as the Standard

On the other hand, when we apply Judeo-Christian ethics, of which Dr. Laura is becoming a champion, we become more than wise, decent, and good. We become fit vessels for God to use to accomplish His work and purposes. As Moses wrote in Deuteronomy 4:5-8:

> See, I have taught you decrees and laws as the Lord my God commanded me, so that you may follow them in the land you are entering to take possession of it. Observe

77

them carefully, for this will show your wisdom and understanding to the nations, who will hear about all these decrees and say, "Surely this great nation is a wise and understanding people." What other nation is so great as to have their gods near them the way the Lord our God is near us whenever we pray to him? And what other nation is so great as to have such righteous decrees and laws as this body of laws I am setting before you today?

In the Old Testament, the Jewish nation was set apart by God through the Law given on Mount Sinai. They were greatly blessed, and they prospered when they carefully followed God's standard and fared poorly when they did not. But more importantly, when they were being faithful to that moral standard, they were in a position to help other nations find and understand God. A holy God. A wise God. A loving God. A just God. A compassionate and merciful God. How different from the gods their neighbors worshiped by burning their babies alive in human sacrifices. So Israel was called to be a servant of Jehovah, to declare the one true and living God and show the excellence of His moral standard to the world.

In the New Testament, Christians are called to do the same for those around them. Jesus called the people of God the "light of the world" and the "salt of the earth"; others are supposed to see our good works and glorify God (Matthew 5:13-16). They are supposed to see the life and teaching of the Christ who "declared" God to the world and who now lives in us who believe in Him.

Bible critics may debate the inspiration of Scripture, but there is no denying the power of God's Word—and its *staying* power—as the premier moral standard of the ages. Neither is there any disputing the quality of individual, family, and community life it produces within those who actually live by it. This is the wisdom that has become Dr. Laura's *standard* prescription. "Take two commandments and fax me in the morning."

"It Simplifies My Life"
One of my favorite questions to ask in a Bible study is, "What do you

cherish most about your faith in the Scriptures?" The simplest and most profound answer I've ever received was from "Grandma Ina Mae," one of the wisest, gentlest, and most loving Christian women I've ever had the privilege to know. She died a year ago, but many of her lessons will be with me for the rest of my life. Hers was the first hand up that Sunday morning, and her answer was moving and instructive.

"What I appreciate most about my faith in God and my confidence in His Word is that it simplifies my life!" She explained that she didn't always understand why people acted the way they did, even members of her own family or her friends. She didn't always know why God said this or did that. She didn't always know why life unfolded the way it did. She just knew that her Father knew best, and she was therefore happy to make her decisions based on His definitions of right and wrong. As an older woman, she had met and known hundreds of people throughout her life who had done things their way and those who had done things God's way. Invariably, the ones who were most content, appreciated what they had, dealt best with adversity and suffering, were the most successful with their marriages and child rearing, and contributed most to their community were those who lived by God's standards.

Nothing points to the complications that set in when we scrap God and His ethical standards more markedly than the "moral dilemmas" presented to Dr. Laura. One caller, deeming herself a "religious person," should have had an easier time finding the solution to her problem than she did.

This young woman was engaged to marry her boyfriend, whom she'd been dating for about a year-and-a-half. He had two children from a previous marriage. She knew the children, and they were happy about the whole thing. So far so good.

Dr. Laura: So he's shopping for a ring.
Caller: And he thinks that once we're engaged, I should move in with him while we plan the wedding.
Dr. Laura: And you think . . .
Caller: Well, my question is, is that a bad idea?

Dr. Laura: No, I said, "You think . . ."

Caller: I'm not sure how I think, I don't . . .

Dr. Laura: Why don't you take a moment out and cogitate; I'll sit here and hum.

Caller: It doesn't feel completely right, but I can't come up with an explanation why.

Dr. Laura: OK, would we have to show that it was life or death, or what would be a good reason why?

Caller: Well, it does help us save money for the wedding.

Dr. Laura: And we *know* that money *is* the most important criterion for making decisions about such things.

Caller: Well, I don't want to jeopardize our long-term success, but I can't come up with a logical reason why.

Dr. Laura: Can I give you one?

Caller: Yes! Please!

Dr. Laura: You guys obviously aren't religious, so I can't go there . . .

Caller: (objecting) Yes, we are! But . . .

Dr. Laura: Well, then, that's a slam-dunk. It's not spiritually correct.

Caller: But for what logical reason though?

Dr. Laura: Can you give me a logic for holiness?

Caller: No, I can't come up with one.

Dr. Laura: You said you were religious. I don't know what that means—every six months you go to church, or do you actually think about these things? Now, I know that I'm pushing you now, but I hate when people throw around, "I'm religious."

Caller: Well, we're both religious in the sense that we are of the same religion.

Dr. Laura: That means *nothing!* That sounds like, "We're both from Anaheim." You know like, so what?

Caller: (laughing) . . . OK.

Dr. Laura: What is religion supposed to do? This is good, I'm enjoying this, so don't freak out on me—stay with me on this. What is religion supposed to do for you? I mean, why bother? Sunday, I'd rather go shopping!

Caller: Well, it keeps me . . . sane.

Dr. Laura: No, psychiatry does that.

Caller: (laughing) I don't know, help me out, Dr. Laura.

Dr. Laura: This is your life! How do you not know this?

Caller: I just know that God has been my Savior and I . . .

Dr. Laura: What does that mean? OK. Assume for a moment that God is your Savior, because I have no idea what *you* mean by that. If somebody is your Savior—you don't owe them? Don't you owe something to someone who has given you such a gift as . . . saviorism?

Caller: Oh, absolutely

Dr. Laura: Well, what do you think you owe God?

Caller: (hesitantly) Uh . . . to live by His Word?

Dr. Laura: OK. What else?

Caller: OK . . . I'm trying to follow where you're going, to see how this relates to living together . . .

Dr. Laura: You . . . you can't see any leap? OK, let's go back. God is your Savior. A savior means saving from something. What have you been saved from?

Caller: Again . . . uh . . . (struggling with the answer) . . . just from going insane.

Dr. Laura: God is your savior from going insane?

Caller: Yes (laughing good-naturedly).

Dr. Laura: You don't get a lot out of services, do you? As I said, since this is *totally* not your venue, let's go somewhere else.

Caller: OK.

Dr. Laura: Do you think it's in the best interest of children to role model for them since, number one, they've already had two parents not keep their covenant and stay together, that you guys would be flippant about your covenant and shack up? Is this helpful to children to cultivating a sense of hopefulness about their relationships when they get older?

Caller: Well . . . I think that . . .

Dr. Laura: Can I have a yes or a no?

Caller: (long pause) Of course I want the children to have a healthy role model, and that's why we're not living together right now.

Dr. Laura: And that's why it should stay that way. But you wanted a logical, practical reason—that's one.

Caller: OK.

Dr. Laura: It would give the kids a further impression that commitment is frivolous.

Caller: Even though we're engaged?

Dr. Laura: That's correct. A lot of engaged people don't get married. Engagement isn't the commitment. It's an intention to commit. Marriage is the commitment. They've already seen that. That commitment can mean nothing.

Caller: That's true.

Dr. Laura: So, do you want to add to their cynicism?

Caller: No, I do not.

Dr. Laura: Then you will not do that. Is that a good reason?

Caller: Yes, that works for me.

Dr. Laura: OK. Now, I think you need to go to church, sit with your minister, and ask, "From what has God saved me?" When you have a relationship with somebody, you have to understand that it goes in two directions. If God is your Savior, then do you not owe God? If you do owe God, what do you owe Him? Ultimately, what we give Him is our behaviors.

I've always thought that was one of the most amazing and instructive (not to mention depressing) calls Dr. Laura has ever had. It exposes the false notion that people can merely profess to be religious and still benefit from that faith. God cannot simplify our lives until (1) we seek a fuller knowledge of His standard, and (2) take it seriously.

I sometimes wonder which Bibles are read the least—the ones

in homes all over the country or those Gideon Bibles in hotel rooms? Sadly enough, that actually might be a toss-up. I've seen far too many Bibles used only as photo archives, flower presses, or places in which to record birth, death, and wedding information. The actual wisdom part remains untapped.

| **"Everyone Did What Was Right in His Own Eyes"** | But a careless, indifferent, and willful ignorance of standards is not the only way to neutralize |

them. We usually just flat-out reject them! Decide (as most of our nation seems to have done) that we want to do things our way. That's what many of the ancient Israelites were doing according to the book of Judges.

One example of how whole families and whole communities are diminished and fragmented, weakened and divided by failure to adhere to an objective ethical standard is demonstrated very well in chapters 17 and 18. A major theme of Judges is stated in 17:6 (KJV): "In those days there was no king in Israel, but every man did that which was right in his own eyes." So the individual's rejection of God's law was made even worse, and in part caused, by a lack of good moral leadership (déjà vu!).

This is a story of everyone "doing their own thing," "letting it all hang out," and "stepping to the beats of their own little drummers." A family whose lives and relationships were growing incredibly complicated because they were ignoring, flatly rejecting, disobeying God's standards. It was family against family and neighbor against neighbor. Those who should have been closely knit friends, neighbors, and loved ones, were all hurting each other. Dejection, discouragement, and division everywhere.

I was going to highlight some key verses and discuss the main points after asking you to read Judges 17 and 18 for yourself but then I thought, maybe I can get the main points across "Dr. Laura–style." How would this have all played out had Micah been able to call Dr. Laura on the phone? How would that conversation have gone?

Micah: Hi, Dr. Laura, I'm Micah.

Dr. Laura: Oh, I like that name! What does it mean?

Micah: It means, "Who is like Jehovah?"

Dr. Laura: Oh, what a wonderful name, and a lot to live up to! Your family must be very spiritual. How can I help you today?

Micah: Well, uh, er, uh

Dr. Laura: Just spit it out.

Micah: It all started when I stole from my mom.

Dr. Laura: (groan) You stole from your own mother? The one who bore you, nursed you, took care of you all these years? What kind of gratitude is that?

Micah: Well, I'm not uh, proud of it.

Dr. Laura: I should think not. How much did you steal?

Micah: 1,100 shekels of silver.

Dr. Laura: What does that mean in English?

Micah: About a 150 grand, but I gave it all back!

Dr. Laura: Well, that's a step in the right direction. Was your conscience getting to you?

Micah: Well, actually, my mom sort of put a curse on the thief, and since I'm kinda superstitious . . .

Dr. Laura: What? You ripped off your mom and you're not even sorry about it? You just didn't want a curse hanging over your head?

Micah: Well, I uh, I do wish I hadn't done it but now . . .

Dr. Laura: I'm curious, Micah. If your mom hadn't put a curse on the thief, would you still have returned the money?

Micah: The thing is . . .

Dr. Laura: Could I just have a yes or a no, please?

Micah: I don't know.

Dr. Laura: We don't do "I don't knows" around here. Try again!

Micah: (long pause) I, uh, that's really hard to say, I hadn't given it much thought.

Dr. Laura: Uh huh. Well, what is your question for me, little Mr. "Who is like Jehovah?"

Micah: Well, my mom was so thrilled that I 'fessed up. She spent over 200 shekels, I mean over 25 grand, to have some idols made just for me,

Dr. Laura: You can't see me 'cause this is radio, but my jaw is on the floor! Let me get this straight, your mother, the one who gave you that name, spent a fourth of her fortune on idolatry? She buys idols and graven images to show appreciation for her twit son who only confessed to his crime 'cause he was scared something might happen to him? Does the phrase "Ten Commandments" mean anything to your family at all?

Micah: Well yeah, we have them written right on our door posts but . . .

Dr. Laura: Well, sounds like you pretty much have them all broken by heart. Thou shalt not have any other gods before me, thou shalt not make idols or graven images—bowing down and worshiping them. Honor your father and mother. Don't steal. Don't covet. Ya know, God gave those to us for a reason!

Micah: You're right, you're right.

Dr. Laura: Though with a mother like that, I guess you can't expect the apple to fall very far from the tree.

Micah: Anyway, I appointed my son to be a priest so we could kinda set up our own little worship center here. I also consecrated an itinerant Levite to help out.

Dr. Laura: And I'm sure they're both descendants of Aaron, right?

Micah: What?

Dr. Laura: Oh do go on, I'm fascinated! Disgusted, but fascinated.

Micah: Well, some of my own countrymen, my neighbors from Dan—600 of them armed to the teeth—ripped me off . . .

Dr. Laura: (sigh) Sauce for the goose . . .

Micah: . . . stole all my idols, and talked my priest into joining them. Said it was a big promotion.

Dr. Laura: (with growing impatience) Sir, what is your question for me?

Micah: Well, would it be morally right for me to go after them and, you know, get my stuff back?

Dr. Laura: Sounds like suicide to me. Why would you want to run that kind of risk against a small army?

Micah: (indignantly) Well, what they did to me wasn't right!

Dr. Laura: Oh, so now all of a sudden you have an attack of the righties. You can dance to any tune you want to but you want everyone else to keep the commandments! Where was your regard for righteousness when it came to God, when it came to your mother, when it came to creating your own little priesthood there?

Micah: But, but, they took everything from me. What else do I have left?

Dr. Laura: (rapping knuckles sharply on the mike) HellOOOO! What do you have left? How can you even dare to ask that? Sir, I'd keep a sharp eye out for lightning storms if I were you! You are a child of God, living in this land flowing with milk and honey, Jehovah (remember the namesake thing?) is there just waiting to bless you and you have the effrontery to ask *What do I have left?* (Double groan). I've heard enough.

Dr. Laura: Samson, welcome to the program, What's that? You're having a bad hair day?!? Oh, it's all your girlfriend's fault, is it? Look, don't even go there, oy veh!

Standards Are a Compass, Not a Weather Vane

Jesus told us, "Heaven and earth will pass away, but my words will never pass away" (Matthew 24:35). The prophet Isaiah said the same thing in the Old Testament:

The grass withers and the flowers fall,
  but the word of our God stands forever. (Isaiah 40:8)

And this is pretty much what Dr. Laura upholds, as the following monologue underscores.

D_____ just faxed me and what she said is a positive saying of the day. This is a concept that a vast, huge number of our society does not believe in, and it's probably the main thing that gets me so much negative press. Here it is. It's by Edward Laymen.

It says, "Principle, particularly moral principle, can never be a weather vane spinning around this way and that, with the shifting winds of expediency. Moral principle is a compass forever fixed and forever true."

Now I have come to believe in and I extol that virtue. That gets me in a lot of trouble. Probably the single thing that gets me in trouble. And you can tell that because whenever I read press attacks on me—or even descriptions of me—they don't argue a point. They just get mean. However, the principles remain. And so do I.

And so does God's Word.

What We Need Today

We've already seen what following standards based on our "imperial selves" has brought us. Our situation is an eerie echo of the state of Israel in Hosea's time.

Hear the word of the Lord, you Israelites,
because the Lord has a charge to bring
against you who live in the land:
"There is no faithfulness, no love, no acknowledgment
of God in the land.
There is only cursing, lying and murder,
stealing and adultery;
they break all bounds,
and bloodshed follows bloodshed.

Because of this the land mourns,
and all who live in it waste away. . . ." (Hosea 4:1-3)

There's nothing new going on in our country. We're just not letting a superior and objective ethical standard—God's—simplify our lives. When a nation loves and respects God and lives by His moral standards, it prospers. Why wouldn't it? God calls us to love, honor, and cherish our families, our neighbors, and the foreigner who dwells among us.

Now, wouldn't that simplify a lot of things? So would simply following the Golden Rule: "In everything, do to others what you would have them do to you, for this sums up the Law and the Prophets" (Matthew 7:12). What would this nation, our communities, and our homes be like if we actually applied the Golden Rule? Think about it. Before we say or do anything, we need to ask ourselves if we would want anyone to say or do this to us. If the answer is no, we simply refrain. If everyone did this, there would be no gossip, no theft, no lying, no infidelity, no road rage, no etc., etc., etc. Pretty scary, huh?

This order of things—putting God first, others second, and ourselves last—is the quintessential definition of true humility and the exact opposite of self-centeredness (there's that word again). The Lord calls us to a kind, gentle, and benevolent spirit. He also does not want us to take sin and injustice lightly. While forgiveness and mercy are always encouraged by God, that which is wrong and harmful to people should be dealt with firmly.

To some, promoting and holding others to God's standards sounds awfully self-righteous. Who died and made us God, anyway? That very question has been asked of Dr. Laura, who answered with honesty and humility . . . and humor.

Somebody asked me in an interview today, this morning, on the phone, about standards. You know, where do I get off? It was asked sort of tongue-in-cheek, you know, a devil's advocate kind of thing. It wasn't hostile, it was a wonderful interview. "Where do you get off telling people how to live their life?"

I said, *"I'm only reiterating three thousand years of wisdom."* I don't have the brains to come up with this stuff myself. That's God. I just reiterate and bang on pots to get your attention. While I've been asked that several times, one time it was asked with hostility. "Who died and made you God?!?" . . . But you don't have to be God to reiterate God's words. That's the point of the Bible given to us. It was given. It was a gift. And I do look at it as a gift—except for the no bacon part. I'm still struggling to find the blessing in that!

Bacon or no bacon, God's standards are a blessed gift! Moses' challenge to us to receive it and follow it is as penetrating today as it was at the time he wrote it:

See, I set before you today life and prosperity, death and destruction. For I command you today to love the Lord your God, to walk in his ways, and to keep his commands, decrees and laws; then you will live and increase, and the Lord your God will bless you. . . .

But if your heart turns away and you are not obedient, and if you are drawn away to bow down to other gods and worship them [which would include ourselves], I declare to you this day that you will certainly be destroyed. . . .

Now choose life, so that you and your children may live and that you may love the Lord your God, listen to his voice, and hold fast to him. For the Lord is your life. (Deuteronomy 30:15–20)

Life and death. It doesn't get much simpler than that.

In My Never-to-Be-Humble Opinion

I'm a tiny bit in mourning today—I really am—and I'm not going to spend a lot of time dwelling on this. The state of New Jersey has now said any two bodies can adopt a kid—a shacking-up couple, lesbian couple, homosexual couple. So I guess kids don't need a mommy and a daddy; they don't need people who are committed in a covenant. They just need bodies around. . . .

Kids don't matter; it's how all the adults feel—that's the direction we've been going in. The adults' feelings matter, and everybody is really making the point that fathers don't count, mothers don't count, coming from a committed family doesn't count—nothing counts. I thought we might get over this moronicy from the sixties. . . . Our society is in abysmal disarray. Unbelievable. So, I'm in mourning; that's all I want to say about it. I'm too disgusted. Too thoroughly disgusted.

Dr. Laura, December 1997

Strong Convictions and Intellectual Honesty

Often, when people ask Dr. Laura for advice or when she launches into a monologue, she frequently prefaces her remarks with, "In my never-to-be-humble opinion." She says it tongue-in-cheek, because she knows that people don't generally associate her straightforward—even brusque—responses with humility. One day she said with a chuckle, "I may be wrong, but at least I'm never uncertain!" She holds her convictions with great strength and intensity. She loves to debate with her close friends and colleagues. And if you want to change her mind on something, know that it can be done—but you'd better bring your lunch, because it's not going to be quick, easy, painless, or quiet!

For all of her certitude, and in spite of the way she comes across, longtime listeners know that Dr. Laura does have an open mind. If you present a logical and well-reasoned case, she will give serious thought to it. And because of that, she has radically changed the way she views the world and her place in it over the years. She has also changed her mind about many controversial social issues that have polarized conservatives and liberals—both political and religious.

Twenty years ago, the odds of Dr. Laura ever being

- a sincere believer in God and a practicing religious person,
- one who holds the opinion that homosexual partnerships undermine the family,
- a critic of feminism (and hated foe of feminists), or
- antiabortion

would have been remote—not even worth calculating. However, the fact that she has changed her views on these and other important issues demonstrates an intellectual honesty—and humility—that is both refreshing and rare.

Let's face it. We all like to think we're right, don't we? We all tend to cling to our opinions (even the ill-informed ones) like piranhas on a pot roast. But we need to keep an open mind, an honest heart, and an awareness of our own limitations—we need humility. A preacher once reminded his congregation, "We are all going to die not knowing just about everything!" How true! We all have much to learn and need to spend our lives continually studying, thinking, and growing.

Traditional Marriage and Family

Daily, "Mother" Laura makes impassioned and well-reasoned pleas for society to return to the traditional, two-parent home; for husbands and wives to take their commitment as seriously as a lifelong covenant demands. She has learned, through her journey into conservative Judaism, that the biblical precepts concerning God's design for the family are simple and straightforward: "For this reason a man will leave his father and mother and be united to his wife, and they will become one flesh" (Genesis 2:24). In the New Testament, Jesus was once asked, "Is it lawful for a man to divorce his wife for any and every reason?" (Mathew 19:3). His answer was no (the only exception being infidelity), and He drew His reasoning from Genesis 2:24—God's ideal.

God's desire is for us to live in sanctified, permanent, monogamous relationships composed of one man and one woman. Two becoming one flesh. A plural unity. A family. He intended that we rear children in that stable, God-focused environment so that they can, in turn, repeat the process with their own children. When I refer to the "ideal," I am describing the conditions that most frequently, consistently, and dependably produce the most beneficial effects.

Of course, there are painful exceptions to God's ideal. We live in an imperfect world. Sometimes husbands or wives see their relationship absolutely shattered by infidelity, by severe mental cruelty or physical abuse, or by drugs and alcohol. It's too much to expect a spouse and children to live under many of these circumstances and divorce might be occasionally unavoidable.

Other types of disasters such as accidental death, crime, or wartime casualty sometimes strips a home of one, or even both parents. My own father died when he was only 30 because of a congenital heart defect. I was seven at the time. Less than two years later my mother was killed in a car accident. A year after my grandparents adopted my two sisters and me, my grandfather died. My grandmother was left to raise us by herself and it was a hard road to hoe. Fortunately, she received compassionate and loving help from the local church we were members of and we managed. None of this changes God's ideal however, nor the obvious benefits that derive from it.

But it is one thing to struggle through calamity that is beyond our ability to control, and it is quite another to do what modern society is doing—intentionally "pioneering" alternatives to what God put into place "in the beginning."

Traditional Family "Alternatives"

What do we do, though, with those whose agenda is to dismantle God's ideal for marriage and family? Politically correct groups constantly administer large doses of euphemistic anesthesia to dull our intellectual and moral awareness. They proclaim "traditional family alternatives," and it doesn't merely sound harmless, it sounds downright virtuous! In the midst of its prosperity and hedonism, our nation is rushing to validate relationships we once knew were unnatural and principles we once understood as immoral. Advocates of gay and lesbian marriages are creating new kinds of "families." Feminists have been redefining gender roles. And our educational and political leaders have been striving to make all of this acceptable as a new cultural norm. To accomplish such agendas, however, requires a complete change in ethical standards (not to mention an obvious disregard for our own biology!). Changes that are irreconcilable with the traditional Judeo-Christian standard our nation was built upon.

For example, society used to disapprove of shacking up. You ask the average person today, as Dr. Laura often does, "Why don't you just go ahead and get married?" and they casually reply, "It's just a piece of paper!" Their nonchalance is exceeded only by their ignorance of what marriage is really all about and what it can become for two individuals who are absolutely committed to one another. You want to live together and make babies? Then get married and build a life.

Shacking up has become morally acceptable, however, and there is "nothing wrong with it." More than that, today it is proudly presented as a legitimate "alternative" to the traditional family.

In the same way, divorce was not a prevalent—certainly not a desired—option. You marry someone, commit yourself to someone, then work it out! Marriage was for life. Now that divorce has become as easy as it is commonplace, now that divorce has been sanctioned in the new order of today's ethics, it, too, is enthusiastically promoted as a viable "alternative"—to the detriment of traditional marriage, stable communities, a family heritage, children, and more.

And so the institution of marriage has been seriously eroded. It doesn't have the sanctity it once had. It doesn't command the respect it once did. People don't understand the divine and intrinsic glory and honor of it. As a result, it is no longer the bedrock for good and stability in our society that it once was.

I heard a comedian on TV say one time that somebody gave him a humidifier for Christmas and another friend gave him a dehumidifier. So he put them both in the same room, plugged them in, and let them "fight it out." That is the problem with all of these "alternatives" to the traditional family. They are fighting it out with each other because they cannot peacefully coexist.

That's why the "alternatives" discussed in this chapter are not viable for our nation. And that isn't just Dr. Laura's opinion or mine. Our nation has been trying them out for thirty years now and look where we are. Parents, kids, families, and society in general are all much worse off. The much-anticipated enlightenment that was supposed to attend our post-Christian era is already showing itself for what it really is: *endarkenment.*

Issue #1: Homosexuality

Dr. Laura first began to have serious misgivings about homosexuality as an alternative lifestyle when she saw its threat to the traditional family. She received an article about our nation's first lawsuit brought by a heterosexual "domestic partnership" (shack-up couple) who were suing for the same type of domestic benefits that the man's employer, Bell Atlantic, provided for gay and lesbian partners. Reverse discrimination was the big issue. If gay and lesbian couples don't have to be married to receive various benefits, why shouldn't a heterosexual couple be accorded the same "rights"? The guy had a point. The legal implications of this situation made Dr. Laura realize that what many had been saying about the American family being eroded by these "alternative lifestyles" was actually true.

Her musings over the social implications of this article led to some heartfelt, provocative, and personal revelations about the homosexual issue. Revelations made more intense by her religious conversion.

I have to handle something that's very provocative, and I

understand that. I'll do my best to be straight with it (no pun intended). First, I have to take an aside to tell you why I'm bringing this up. For several decades, I . . . went on the air and opened the phones up to everyone—gays, lesbians, straights, all religions, all races—to discuss personal problems and moral issues, and took a lot of grief for doing so. One of the things that was said to me consistently in interviews about this subject was that if you support certain gay rights issues, you will undermine the American family. I said, "That's absurd. What undermines the American family is divorce and drugs and abuse and stuff like that." (Which is not untrue.) But I didn't anticipate this. And this is of great concern. Gays and lesbians, by definition, cannot marry and should not marry—that is my opinion. That's a man and a woman in a covenant with God, and I'm not moving from that. . . .

Where the big problem is for me is that in New York and other places, the laws and regulations to protect long-term, same-sex couples in a committed relationship have been schmeared so that any two people shacking up have the dignity of a married couple. And I have a real problem with that. This is a bad side effect . . . it is going to be a legal problem if you tell two lesbians or two homosexual men that they can have certain rights, but then a man and a woman shacking up can't have the same rights. This has been destructive to the family . . . so actually, because of these legal ramifications, I sit corrected.

This is such a difficulty to struggle with because, I have to tell you, if there's one typical piece of mail I get it's, "How can you say you're a religious Jew if you don't come out and condemn homosexuality when it's clearly in Leviticus" (pause, pained sigh). This is such a difficult subject for me. I'm not the slightest bit intimidated by various gay and lesbian rights groups that don't like the fact that I'm against the New Jersey law, which states that two gays or two lesbians are equal to a husband and wife in adopting a child—I think that's absurd. I think that's catering to the desires of a group instead of the needs of a child to have a mom and a dad. So I take some grief there. Then I take grief from the religious groups because I talk to gays about problems and issues. So I'm not in anyone's camp here.

It is a complex issue for me because I think that in most cases, there is no choice. There is a choice in acting out on it. There's just so many crazy things going on that I want you to know that this is something I am struggling with because I am a religious person, a religious Jew. Part of that brings me to a certain level of compassion, yet not to the extent where, in the case of the New Jersey law, you can think that two women replace a dad. Or that two men replace a mother. That's absurd. I've solidified certain aspects of this and others I haven't, so we don't need the nasty mail. That's what's ironic. I get nasty mail from both sides. You need to take one side so at least half of your mail is positive (sigh). I am in a quandary. There are certain absolute noes and certain absolute yeses, and then there's this whole area where compassion gets me mucked up—I admit it.

Could you sense her sincere angst? I was so affected by her dissertation that I spent the next hour writing a response to her, which I faxed the next day. I did not expect her to read it on the air, but she did. Following is the monologue she delivered as she read my fax. Her comments are in italics.

Nothing like starting the day out with some provocative stuff ... why wait, why work up to it? Just do it, I always say! This is from Pastor Ray McClendon, Church of Christ of Hesperia, California. Um . . . I think this is very interesting. It's an assessment of me, struggling with the homosexuality issue as a religious person. OK?

Dear Dr. Laura,

I have resisted—for the past five years I've been listening and the past three I've been faxing—sending you any thoughts about the homosexual issue. I know thousands of folks already take you to task and get in your face (from both sides) on a regular basis. I've always wanted to accentuate the positive—the common ground we share. But my heart was touched by your honest, sincere expressions of the difficulties you experience wrestling with this thorny issue.

I strongly suspect that your quandary has intensified in direct proportion to the increase of the strength of your conviction that God says *no* at the same time you are holding on to your long-held conviction that folks "are what they are" emotionally, physiologically, sexually, etc. . . . Yet both Old and New Testaments clearly, decisively, and prolifically condemn and denounce homosexuality.

He goes, "I know that was a lousy sentence, but . . ." Oh, that's the kind of sentence I write. My editor hates it, but I love those sentences. They go on and on and on. OK.

It seems to me that there might well be a natural, biological predisposition for some women to be masculine and some men to be feminine. Almost as if that "womb-wash" that triggers the gender change in utero doesn't quite "take."

What this is referring to is that genetically, the apparatus is female. Whether it becomes male is dependent upon the addition of testosterone at the right time and in the right amount. Did you know that? You could be XY and turn out with female genitalia if no testosterone hits at the right time. So we're all destined to become women (ha! ha!). Moving right along.

Too, there might be other factors involved (but as of yet, not understood) that give a man or a woman a predisposition toward same-sex attraction.

Grant that all of this is true! What are we left with? What's the bottom line? If you are going to believe we are made in the image of God and that He is our Creator, then know the following . . .

I'm reading this to you because I find this fascinating, food for thought as they say.

He is certainly aware of the (naturally occurring) anomalies that will occasionally occur (in the case of those who are "born to it"—if indeed that's the case). He is certainly aware of the (arbitrarily created) anomalies that will occasionally occur (in the case of those who choose to lust that way—known to be the case in many instances). Either way, He made no bones about the wrong or sin of lesbianism and homosexuality. Made no allowances for it at all.

I can't argue with that.

That should tell us something. That it is an impulse/condition/reality/temptation that can be controlled and is expected and required by God to be controlled. And is He not a God of supreme compassion?

That's the point I kept bringing up the other day.

Then it would *not* imply a lack of compassion on our part when we stand against it/forbid it/condemn it—as a perversion of God's ideal—no more than it implies a lack of compassion on His part when He stands against it/forbids it/condemns it. No more than it implies a lack of compassion or understanding when we condemn:

Sex outside of marriage (fornication) . . .
because God does, and He's compassionate.
Sex outside of a covenant (adultery) . . .
because God does, and He's compassionate.
Necrophilia . . . because God does, and He's compassionate.
Pedophilia . . . because God does, and He's compassionate. . . .

That one got me.

If sexuality in a committed, monogamous, lifetime relationship is God's ideal (and His expectation); is the ultimate pleasure, joy, and satisfaction we can attain; and if God does not allow for anything else—then we should trust Him that everyone can aspire to that and attain that. It just might be more difficult for some than others. If someone should call your show (and they have from time to time), talking about the intensity of their sex drive, and they were a fornicator, adulterer (or necrophiliac or pedophile, for that matter), would you not simply cite the standard—what God has said and is therefore possible—if they summon the character, courage, conscience (and faith) to choose that? Don't you tell them not to give in to their urges?

Yes. I basically tell them to fight against it.

When it comes to the Ten Commandments, you stand firm and permit no negotiation, no compromise, no dilution, no rationalization. At the same time you maintain your compassion intact. That it is difficult for you when it comes to homosexuality is a commentary on the "subjective," not the "objective." Something you don't have much truck with or tolerate much of from others who call your show.

That's fair.

Like Charles the other day, when you so aptly pointed out that there was a time when true love (personal feelings) were not an issue at all. That marriages were prearranged, foreordained, yet people learned out of necessity to make them not only succeed but succeed magnificently!

The guy's got me, righteously, what can I tell ya?

When we (you and I both) speak of how God's expressed will simplifies our life, we are speaking of the truth that man does not define virtue or vice—God does—and our responsibility as creatures made in His image is to respect and honor His definitions. . . .

I appreciate your not giving up. When you were speaking the other day of the quandary, the confusion, and the difficulty of this issue for you, I couldn't help but think of Jacob wrestling all night, refusing to give up. And because he did not give up, he came away ultimately blessed . . . albeit limping.

(laughing) And because of that, you know, I can't have filet mignon, and I'm still mad about it. If you don't understand what I just said, get yourself a rabbi. All right. I think that is probably the best essay on this—to me—that I have ever received that makes sense. That's why I wanted to read it. Now I have to figure out what to do with it, and still sleep.

When I saw Dr. Laura in her office a couple weeks later, the first thing she said was, "Did you hear me read your fax on the air?"

"Yes," I replied, "I almost fell out of my chair." I told her the church office had received calls from all over the country about it, and it had been well-received by a lot of folks. I ended our brief conversation by saying, "I think God's been dragging you kicking and screaming to this conclusion for a long time."

She just smiled.

Sensitivity *and* Truth

As Dr. Laura has come to terms with the Judeo-Christian ethic on homosexual practice, some of her listeners have more than noticed. They have become concerned. She published one letter in her magazine that someone had anonymously written to her voicing his concern. It had the heading, "You Can Be Moral AND Gay." While I'm sure she had several reasons for publishing it, one was that it was written with a courteous and congenial tone and displayed a good attitude. Dr. Laura believes in giving people a fair hearing. Here's a short excerpt from that letter:

> Dear Dr. Laura,
> First of all, I would like to thank you for the impact you have had on my life. You have guided me in my quest to become a moral, responsible adult. I agree with 90-something percent of what you say. But I feel compelled to share my differences with you on one important issue—homosexuality. I know you've struggled with this issue, and I've noticed your views becoming more conservative. Please, I ask you, don't lose the compassion that earned you a special place in my heart a few years ago. You see, I am gay.

The individual made several valid points in the letter, but his principal theme was that you can be both moral *and* gay. His admonition to Dr. Laura concerning moral gays was not to "lose them by using antigay rhetoric."

As a Christian, I believe that there is no place for hateful invective or bashing of people when you are trying to work through differences. Respect is vital. Dr. James Dobson's June 1998 *Focus on the Family* newsletter, for example, models the balance between empathy toward homosexuals and the Scripture's truth concerning homosexuality and how the homosexual agenda undermines the traditional family: "We believe every human being is precious to God and is entitled to acceptance and respect. There is great suffering among homosexuals, and it is our desire to show compassion and concern for those caught in that lifestyle."

Sensitivity, however, can become enablement if it shies away from Scripture's truth. Homosexual sex itself is against nature, nature's God, and God's Scripture.

> Do not lie with a man as one lies with a woman; that is detestable. (Leviticus 18:22)

In Romans 1, the Apostle Paul refers to gay and lesbian sex as one manifestation of what happens when humankind rebels against God and serves the creature (himself) rather than the Creator:

> Therefore God gave them over in the sinful desires of their hearts to sexual impurity for the degrading of their bodies with one another. They exchanged the truth of God for a lie, and worshiped and served created things rather than the Creator—who is forever praised. Amen.
>
> Because of this, God gave them over to shameful lusts. Even their women exchanged natural relations for unnatural ones. In the same way the men also abandoned natural relations with women and were inflamed with lust for one another. Men committed indecent acts with other men, and received in themselves the due penalty for their perversion. (Romans 1:24-27)

The simple truth is, the Judeo-Christian Scriptures define homosexual practice as wrong, just as it pronounces many other types of illicit sex as wrong. So while gays can and often do perform many moral acts, they cannot be moral at the point they are engaging in homosexual behavior.

A Word about Homophobia

None of this is gay-bashing or homophobia. When I'm teaching against fornication, for example, I'm not "hetero-bashing." I'm just making a simple statement of conviction based on clear moral precepts. Since Jews and Christians accept God and His Scriptures as their moral authority, we can't say this is OK when God has said it is not.

Homophobia, by the way, is one of the worst, most imprecise words ever coined. In popular usage, it has come to mean fear of homosexual people and their lifestyle. If people do not approve of homosexual activity, if they contend that homosexual orientation is not a civil rights issue, they are labeled homophobic. If we say, "I don't believe men should have sex with men and neither should women have sex with other women," we are branded as homophobes. That is, we are deemed to fear homosexuals.

This is not true. Those who accept Scripture as the standard for right and wrong merely contend that homosexual sex is morally wrong just as sex with people you're not married to is wrong and immoral.

What if we used the homosexual community's logic in regard to other immoral sexual behaviors? If someone, for example, does not approve of adultery, would we label him or her "heterophobic"? I am against adults having sex with children. Do I have "pedophobia"? If we believe it's wrong for humans to use animals for sexual purposes, do we have "bestiaphobia"?

What has happened here is that the homosexual community has successfully tarred its opponents with homophobia. Why? Because people who have phobias should not be taken seriously. Just label them and dismiss them. They are clearly the ones with the problem.

God, however, made no provision for homosexual marital arrangements. Homosexuality is a departure from His norm, His ideal. Nature decrees a mom and a dad for procreation and furnishing the appropriate family environment. Gays and lesbians cannot procreate, neither can they raise children in the kind of environment that models what nature requires for the perpetuation of the species. God, the Author of nature, divinely ordained that a mom and a dad live in a committed, covenantal relationship that emphasizes our plural unity in the likeness of Him. "Male and female he created them." Not "Male and male he created them." Not "Female and female he created them."

Issue #2: Feminism Feminism of the more extreme variety has certainly done more than its fair share to destroy the American family in the last thirty years. If alternative family and domestic partnerings of various kinds, genders, and levels of commitment have been attacking the traditional family from the outside, feminists have been attacking from the inside.

NOW (the National Organization for Women) was built on the idea that women should abandon their homemaking and child rearing to enter the workplace. Once you are economically independent of men, once you are in full command of your own sexuality, then, sister, you have truly reached the promised land!

But what has this brought us? We have a higher rate of multiple divorces and remarriages, and the rate of shack-up failures is even higher than that. Less commitment than ever, but more unwanted pregnancies and unwanted children (if they escape abortion), more venereal disease, more HIV, and less help with children.

Here are just some of the lies that radical feminists have hawked and our society has bought.

- You can have everything—career, marriage, family, social life, and anything else your heart desires— with absolutely no negative consequences.
- Traditional religion is a patriarchal system, so it denigrates women.
- While marriage is fine, divorce is OK too. There are no lasting consequences for the women and children.
- The greatest legacy women can leave is to do the same things men do, prove they are as "good" as men—equal by being the same.

Every day Dr. Laura issues a wake-up call against this philosophy that she once ardently embraced. Here is just one of many examples:

I was interviewed the other day, and they asked me about

my religion, my Orthodox conversion. "Gee, why did I do that? Isn't that fundamentalist, like fundamentalist Christians . . . fundamentalist Jews? Aren't you all sexist?" I just started laughing. I couldn't think of anything funnier than the sexist remark. Let's go into the stores and look at all the clothes. Let's go out into society and observe the mentality which is unisex. Men and women are completely different but should be treated exactly the same? Excuse me! My arms don't work when I'm near a door if there's a man there—that's his job. That's his way of showing respect.

I'm sorry, there are differences. In Judaism, women are viewed as being more spiritual than men . . . I sorta like the idea that my womanhood and my femininity is exalted, and I'm not considered the same as a man (superior actually [chuckles], but moving right along). So I don't get the unisex mentality. It has so robbed women of the truth, of the very things which we all seek, which is, we want to be feminine, we want to be respected, we want to mother our children, we want to have healthy relationships. It's not unisex.

How are many women responding to Dr. Laura's stand against radical feminism? Here's one example.

Dear Dr. Laura:
I heard you discussing NOW (National Organization for I Don't Know What Kind of Women) on your program a couple weeks ago and would like to say, *"Hooray for you!"*

I am sick and tired of these women speaking for all of us and calling us "sisters." I have a college degree from a liberal arts university, have taken courses toward a master's, work full-time as the director of a statewide organization, and am involved in several business and professional associations. However, NOW thinks I'm a buffoon because I don't adhere to their enlightened philosophies. You see, I'm married, and I like it. I don't feel oppressed at all by my loving, caring, sensitive husband. I prefer adoption over abortion and mom over nanny. If God blesses us with a child, I would be honored to care for it. I could go on and on.

NOW is an extreme, anti-God, antimen, and anti-family organization. I would no sooner associate with them than with a rabid dog. Unfortunately, whenever women's issues arise, the media calls on a NOW representative to give us the view. Thank you for being the voice of all the other women out here in the real world— we need people like you!

Womanhood in general is one of the more frequent topics of discussion on Dr. Laura's program. No surprise there. Women comprise a majority of her callers. In the midst of their moral dilemmas, Dr. Laura speaks with each of them about summoning the three C's they need to start setting things right.

For the most part, these women are striving to become better women. They have come to know through personal experience that foolish or immoral choices lead to unhappiness and emptiness. Many have had poor upbringings, have been taught relative ethics, and their hearts are aching. They yearn for real solutions to their problems.

So Dr. Laura tells the troubled, unhappy, and often tearful women what they really need to be doing with their lives. Accept responsibility for themselves. Quit playing the victim. Begin doing meaningful things. If single, then finish their education. Become independent, self-sufficient, and responsible for themselves before seeking a relationship so that they can bring a whole and healthy person into that relationship. If married, then prioritize their commitments to their husband and children. Make worthwhile contributions to their family, community, and church.

Dr. Laura makes it clear day in and day out that there are no shortcuts to a purposeful life. If you want a meaningful life, then you must do meaningful things. While so many of Dr. Laura's major themes and issues are absolutely biblical, nowhere is there more overlap than right here.

The Scriptural Ideal

Several marvelous examples in both Old and New Testaments present God's picture of what women can be. Proverbs 31 is perhaps, more than any other biblical text, the crown jewel in the woman's scriptural diadem. There God ascribes great power and dignity to worthy women, presents a woman's life as a high calling. Such women deserve our honor and our respect, because they earn it. Their accomplishments are significant and far-reaching and grow out of who they are as wise, good, and hardworking people. The following rendering of Proverbs 31 is from the *New Jerusalem Bible*.

> The truly capable woman—who can find her?
>   She is far beyond the price of pearls.
> Her husband's heart has confidence in her,
>   from her he will derive no little profit.
> Advantage and not hurt she brings him
>   all the days of her life.
> She selects wool and flax,
>   she does her work with eager hands.
> She is like those merchant vessels,
>   bringing her food from far away.
> She gets up while it is still dark,
>   giving her household their food,
>   giving orders to her serving girls.
> She sets her mind on a field, then she buys it;
>   with what her hands have earned she plants a
>   vineyard.
> She puts her back into her work
>   and shows how strong her arms can be.
> She knows that her affairs are going well;
>   her lamp does not go out at night.
> She sets her hands to the distaff,
>   her fingers grasp the spindle.

She holds out her hands to the poor,
  she opens her arms to the needy.
Snow may come, she has no fears for her
  household, with all her servants warmly clothed.
She makes her own quilts,
  she is dressed in fine linen and purple.
Her husband is respected at the city gates,
  taking his seat among the elders of the land.
She weaves materials and sells them,
  she supplies the merchant with sashes.
She is clothed in strength and dignity,
  she can laugh at the day to come.
When she opens her mouth, she does so wisely;
  on her tongue is kindly instruction.
She keeps good watch on the conduct of her
  household, no bread of idleness for her.
Her children stand up and proclaim her blessed,
  her husband, too, sings her praises:
"Many women have done admirable things,
  but you surpass them all!"
Charm is deceitful, and beauty empty;
  the woman who fears Yahweh is the one to praise.
Give her a share in what her hands have worked
  for, and let her works tell her praises at the city
  gates.
(Proverbs 31:10–31)

While most of the Bible translations use words like *virtuous,* *noble, worthy,* and *excellent* to describe the woman (wife in this context), the New Jerusalem Bible seems to capture the spirit of the Hebrew best. The word *capable* all by itself denotes a force to be reckoned with and is translated throughout the Old Testament with words like *power, strength,* and even *valor.* So God has been saying for thousands of years that women are "perfectly capable"! The abuse and misuse of women has come from ungodly men, not God.

If you reread those verses carefully, you will be impressed with both the intellectual and spiritual qualities of this woman. She has a tremendous work ethic. She is smart, even shrewd, when it comes to business and planning for the future. No one works harder than she does contributing to her family's well-being. She takes good care of her household. She is generous, selfless, and sensitive to others' needs. She has a benevolent spirit. She is reverent and pious. She is a great blessing to her husband and children, who feel indebted to her for what she makes possible for them.

This is God's ideal for women. There is no higher standard of excellence for *true* feminism than the one set forth in the Judeo-Christian Bible. The shrill, worldly, and self-centered feminists of today, who think that scriptural values lead to the subjugation and denigration of women, simply do not understand the Bible. They judge things from a skewed perspective—a perspective, admittedly, for which men themselves need to accept a lot of responsibility.

Time to Share Some Blame

For many years, men have cited—without love or understanding—a passage in Paul's letter to the Ephesians:

> Wives, submit to your husbands as to the Lord. For the husband is the head of the wife as Christ is the head of the church, his body, of which he is the Savior. Now as the church submits to Christ, so also wives should submit to their husbands in everything. (Ephesians 5:22–24)

Men have used this passage to trumpet what they have perceived to be their authority and their superiority over women. And they have done so in the name of God and the Bible. They were wrong. The "headship" of Ephesians 5 has gone to many men's heads and cultivated a "man's home is his castle" mentality. Many men, even professed Christians, have behaved like Neanderthalic oafs. They've left the impression that this is what the Bible teaches. This has served our families and society poorly and has done a grave injustice to true biblical teaching. Unfortunately, in many minds there continues to be a connection between chauvinistic oppression of women and "right-wing Christian fundamentalism." I'll never forget the cartoon strip from the eighties, "Bloom County," by Berke Breathed, that reflected this concept:

The character Otis Oracle is sitting on a park bench, when Milo Bloom comes up to him and observes, "You're looking happy, Mr. Oracle." To which Otis replies, "I'm ecstatic! I've just been named the Grand Duke of our local Moral Majority chapter!" He felt so inspired he told Milo, "Know what I think I'll do? Go right home and dominate my wife!" Milo is shouting "Rapture!" with outstretched arms.

The next thing you know, Otis is walking through the front door shouting, "Wife! I am home! Fix me a steak!" The wife retorts from the other room, "Fix it yourself, Mr. Moral Majority. I'm tired." Otis comes back with, "Wife . . . your moral responsibility is to serve your husband, and I want dinner served now . . . do you hear me? NOW!!" Next thing you know, Otis is in the kitchen with an apron on reading the back of a TV dinner that says, "Place tray on center rack. Peel back corner of foil to expose tater tots . . ."

So men are largely responsible for creating one extreme, which, in turn, has led to the other extreme that now manifests itself in modern feminism. Over the years, we have been emphasizing the wrong verse. Immediately after the admonition for wives to submit to their husbands, we find this injunction given to men:

> Husbands, love your wives, just as Christ loved the church and gave himself up for her to make her holy, cleansing her by the washing with water through the word, and to present her to himself as a radiant church, without stain or wrinkle or any other blemish, but holy and blameless. In this same way, husbands ought to love their wives as their own bodies. He who loves his wife loves himself. (Ephesians 5:25–28)

The church, made up of all true believers, is Christ's bride. And there wasn't anything He would not do for her. Including leaving heaven. Including His own death. Considering the self-sacrificial way Jesus lived and died, can there be any excuse for a husband who claims to be His follower to "lord over" or abuse his wife?

When husbands love their wives with that kind of unselfishness and focus, their leadership in the home becomes a loving and benevolent provision that no woman in her right mind would mind being a part of. That's what the men's movement Promise Keepers is all about, and—ironically, yet predictably—NOW opposes them as well!

Issue #3: Abortion

America is still in denial about abortion. No wonder. Unborn babies look a lot like newborn babies. Unborn babies are growing and developing all the while they are in the womb, being nourished by their mothers, just like newborn babies grow and develop as they are nourished by their mothers. At just a few weeks old, unborn babies have their own fingers, toes, brains, heart, etc., just like a newborn baby. Which is probably why *fetus* is Latin for baby. I don't know if you knew that. At the moment of conception, the genetic code of this new life is complete. And it's not the genetic code of the mother for the simple reason that the fetus's body is not the mother's body. It's just dependent on her body in the earliest stages of life. "Reproductive freedom"—more euphemistic anesthesia—should be confined to doing what you wish with your own genetic code, not somebody else's. A fetus is its own entity.

Women who have abortions have in their hearts an emotional time bomb just waiting to go off. When the day comes for them to bring a *child* to term, and they feel the *baby* moving around inside of them—the one they've decided not to abort—then the magnitude of what they have done will sink horribly and painfully deep into their hearts.

Why else would an extensive *U.S. News and World Report* article, "Abortions in America," be subtitled, "So Many Women Have Them, So Few Talk about Them"?[1] In this well-documented and thoroughly researched article, the reporters pointed out that 43 percent of American women will have an abortion in their lifetime. This makes abortion nearly as common as divorce, three times more common than breast cancer, and more than twice as many women get abortions as get college degrees. The article states, "It would mean that 25 years after Roe v. Wade, abortions are safe, legal, and not rare."

Yet the article points out that women are reticent to discuss having had abortions. Some even declined to be interviewed because their mothers would have to be told. Then they worried about their friends and coworkers finding out. *Why the guilt?* I wondered. Why haven't many women made peace with themselves yet? Why do some abortion clinics require counseling? Why do some people go to a clinic out of state to avoid the counseling? Why is the psychology of abortion so complicated, according to abortion clinics? If abortion is so common nowadays, if we've worked so hard at removing the moral stigma from it, and if it's just a medical thing, then why do so many women still wrestle with it?

It's because "fetuses" look and feel a lot like "babies" when they're growing inside their mommies. Dr. Laura talks about the day she had her pregnancy confirmed. She was running around joyfully shouting, "I'M PREGNANT! I'M GOING TO HAVE A BABY!" A *baby*.

When Christianity came on the scene in the ancient world, abortion, along with infanticide, declined rapidly. That's because Christians believe we are not, as Dr. Laura puts it, a random assembly of molecules. We are made in the image of God, so there is a sanctity to life—including life in the womb. I didn't have to search for long to find a number of Christian writers from the second, third, and fourth centuries who made that clear.

> Thou shalt not slay the child by procuring abortion; nor, again, shalt thou destroy it after it is born. (Epistle of Barnabas, c. A.D. 150)

> Why then dost thou abuse the gift of God, and fight with His laws, and follow after what is a curse as if a blessing, and make the chamber of procreation a chamber for

murder, and arm the woman that was given for child-bearing unto slaughter? (Chrysostom, c. A.D. 347-407, Homilies on Romans)

Some, when they find themselves with child through their sin, use drugs to procure abortion, and when (as often happens) they die with their offspring, they enter the lower world laden with the guilt not only of adultery against Christ but also of suicide and child murder. (Jerome, c. A.D. 345-419, Letter to Eustochium)

Women also who administer drugs to cause abortion, as well as those who take poisons to destroy unborn children, are murderesses. So much on this subject. (Basil, c. A.D. 330-79, Letter to Amphilochius)

Those guys were nearly as brusque as Dr. Laura on the subject:

Dr. Laura: Welcome to the program.
Caller: Hello.
Dr. Laura: What's on your mind?
Caller: Well, the thing is, is I was engaged, and I got pregnant. My fiancé decided he didn't want to keep the child, and I do want the child.
Dr. Laura: He had no intention of marrying you either? You had a ring and a date?
Caller: We had a date for next summer.
Dr. Laura: You had a vague notion, a vague agreement.
Caller: No, no. It wasn't a vague agreement. Ring and everything.
Dr. Laura: You had a ring and a specific date?
Caller: Not a specific date.
Dr. Laura: OK. He didn't want to have babies ever?
Caller: He . . . we had talked about having children, but he's older than I am, and I have a feeling maybe children

weren't in his plan. I'm sorry, I'm a little . . .

Dr. Laura: You got engaged to a guy and you didn't know if he wanted to have kids?

Caller: No, no. He told me he did, and I guess maybe he didn't. Maybe he thought I would change my mind or something.

Dr. Laura: How old is he?

Caller: He's forty.

Dr. Laura: And you're twenty-three?

Caller: Yeah.

Dr. Laura: It's not typical that forty-year-old men go out with twenty-three-year-old women to start new families.

Caller: I know.

Dr. Laura: All right. So you're pregnant. Are you still pregnant?

Caller: Yes.

Dr. Laura: OK. And what's your question?

Caller: Well, the thing is, he really . . . he's adamant about not having this child.

Dr. Laura: Yeah, he's not marrying you, and he doesn't want to parent this kid.

Caller: No. So I really want this child, but I guess my decision has to be based on reality and whether or not I'm going to do a disservice by having this child.

Dr. Laura: Wait a minute, wait a minute, wait a minute. Are you talking about abortion?

Caller: Yeah.

Dr. Laura: Oh, I see. So we suck it out into little pieces because it's inconvenient. How about we give birth and find a wonderful two-parent family to take care of this child?

Caller: I don't know if I could do that.

Dr. Laura: You can kill it, but you can't wave good-bye? You're an interesting mother. Is that a little too blunt?

Caller: No, no it isn't.

Dr. Laura: But you're telling me you could kill it. That would be easier on you?

Caller: No, it wouldn't.

Dr. Laura: Good. Because I find that a little scary.

Caller: I guess the thing is, is I can't . . .

Dr. Laura: You made a mistake on the man.

Caller: Right.

Dr. Laura: You made a mistake having intercourse outside of a committed relationship. Don't make another mistake by thinking you can handle being mom and dad. And don't make a further mistake sucking this out into a sink and getting on with things.

Caller: Yeah, I guess so.

Dr. Laura: You don't think that would be an interesting memory?

Caller: Well, I guess I'm wondering if I can do it on my own though.

Dr. Laura: Well, do you have somebody to support you so you can stay home and take care of it? Let me make something perfectly clear. Raising kids requires a body to be there, to be loving and attentive and there. Raising a kid is best done for any child when there is a mom and a dad.

Caller: Yeah, I know.

Dr. Laura: So I'm asking you again to consider the possibility of an adoption to a two-parent family who would love and raise this child with a mom and a dad. You know you can stipulate a no-day-care, at-home parent.

Caller: Yeah.

Dr. Laura: You can pick the family.

Caller: I guess I didn't think of that one.

Dr. Laura: Then the kid would have a dad.

Caller: That's true.

Dr. Laura: Better than killing it.

A lot of listeners, including myself, often wonder how many people like that caller actually take Dr. Laura's advice. Oh, she receives a mountain of encouraging faxes and mail every week. But it must seem sometimes like a relatively small amount when we consider how widespread and endemic to our society abortion has become. Watching the news, reading the paper—it just seems that good takes a beating at the hands of evil every day.

I know Dr. Laura well enough to know that sometimes she, too, wonders about how much good she really accomplishes. But at a book signing in Portland, Oregon, she had a marvelous encounter with a thirty-year-old woman who came up to her with a book to sign and a photo with an amazing story behind it.

The woman showed me a photo with herself between two lovely, smiling children—a boy and a girl. I admired the children and remarked how blessed she was to have such a happy, healthy looking family.

She said, "There's something you need to know about them—they're here because of you." I thought she meant they were in Portland instead of somewhere else because of a divorce and custody situation. I have often warned divorced parents against moving away from each other and subjecting their children to the loss of one parent.

That wasn't the case. The children were adopted from different biological moms who both decided not to abort because of listening to my nagging on the radio. This was a stunner.

I again looked into the eyes of those two children in the photo, and truthfully, I didn't know what to say or do because I was so overwhelmed. Those two children will be the continuation of generations of people because their mothers had the courage to give them up and give them life.

To have been the influence on their mothers' character, conviction, and goodness was an honor. Rather than feeling all puffed up that I had done something great, I felt humbled. In fact, I'm crying as I write this.

Sometimes we all feel we are fighting losing battles. But sometimes even losing battles must be fought.

We all need to be thankful for victories like the one Dr. Laura secured with her counsel, because abortion has had such a tremendous impact on our national psyche. It demonstrates just how self-centered, how calloused, we've become. It is unbelievable how many women consider abortion because they "don't think they could give it up once its born" or they "might be doing a disservice to the child." Dr. Laura inevitably responds, "But you can kill it? That's easier? That's better?" Mothers who don't want their babies but don't obtain a partial birth abortion the week before giving birth just toss it into the trash the day after. After all, what's the difference?

All of this underscores just how far we've wandered from our Creator. The early Christian writers I quoted did not conceive their opinions in a vacuum. Respect for God and His Word leads to the same conclusion. The New Testament speaks of life in the womb with the same term, *brephos*, that it speaks of newborn children or infants outside of the womb. In each of the following verses, it's all the exact same Greek word:

- Luke 1:41—"When Elizabeth heard Mary's greeting, the *baby* leaped in her womb."
- Luke 1:44—"As soon as the sound of your greeting reached my ears, the *baby* in my womb leaped for joy."
- Luke 2:16—"So they hurried off and found Mary and Joseph, and the *baby*, who was lying in the manger."
- Luke 18:15—"People were also bringing *babies* to Jesus to have him touch them."
- 2 Timothy 3:15—"From *infancy* you have known the holy Scriptures, which are able to make you wise for salvation through faith in Christ Jesus."
- 1 Peter 2:2—"Like *newborn babies*, crave pure spiritual milk, so that by it you may grow up in your salvation."

The New Testament teaches us that young infants and babies in the womb are the *same*, and the Old Testament speaks of life in the womb as a process of God, one that He is fully aware of and in which He has a hand.

> For you created my inmost being;
>> you knit me together in my mother's womb.
> I praise you because I am fearfully and wonderfully made;
>> your works are wonderful,
>> I know that full well.
> My frame was not hidden from you
>> when I was made in the secret place.
>> When I was woven together in the depths of the earth,
>>> your eyes saw my unformed body.
> All the days ordained for me
>> were written in your book
>> before one of them came to be. (Psalm 139:13-16)

Tampering with life in the womb is tampering with God's own work: Abortion is wrong. Abortion is the ending of life. Abortion is the ending of the life of another. And for that reason abortion is also the ultimate hypocrisy. Only those who are *already* born support it.

Fasten Your Ethical Moorings—A Storm Is Coming

The issues we've examined in this chapter are as controversial as they are important. They are subjects of innumerable monologues, calls, letters, and faxes on Dr. Laura's program. And they are hotly contested, because when you bring the authority of God and the Judeo-Christian ethic to bear in a society that is working so hard to dispense with objective moral authority, it drives people nuts! A huge segment of our society has cut itself loose from our traditional ethical mooring so that we could anchor ourselves—to ourselves. But that's not smart. Any sailor will tell you that you don't anchor a boat to itself! When someone tries to point out the utter insufficiency and folly of that, it becomes a rhetorical free-for-all.

But our debates are difficult and our rhetoric is hot, not because the social issues themselves are all that complex or confusing—God has already weighed in with verdicts on each of them—it's because fewer people nowadays like the decisions He has handed down, so they appeal it to a lower court. Much lower. In this court they get to be their own judge, jury, and star witness, and their own testimony is all they will hear on the matter.

Humanism and atheism have been advancing over theism in our society for the last several generations. Skepticism has been winning out over faith, and we are worshiping the creature rather than the Creator. At the same time, the quality of our civilization is steadily declining.

Dr. Laura knows right from wrong and perceives the harm being done to the nuclear family by each of these issues. While she used to be on the other side of the fence, she now holds forth the Judeo-Christian ethic in each of these areas. We would do well to listen to her. Because a storm is coming.

No, it's already here.

Whirlwinds and Hurricanes

If you look at each one of these events, kids doing drive-by shootings . . . just take one event in the newspaper, on one day, you think, "Bad kid. Shooting each other in schools. Isolated event. Bad kid." So perspective is everything. If you stand back and look at each event, define it, and put it away, you can feel very safe—but you're not. You better stand back and see that it's one raindrop in a hurricane.

Dr. Laura

Family: The Bedrock of Society

Pope John Paul II has said, "As the family goes, so goes the nation and so goes the whole world in which we live."[1] The family is the most fundamental unit in society—society's building block, its bedrock.

Unfortunately, not everyone understands or agrees with this. For example, British novelist Rose Macaulay wrote back in 1950,

As to the family, I have never understood how that fits in with the other ideals—or, indeed, why it should be an ideal at all. A group of closely related persons living under one roof—it is a convenience, often a necessity, sometimes a pleasure, sometimes the reverse. But who first exalted it as admirable, an almost religious ideal?[2]

Who exalted the family as an ideal? God did! It is His design—

the natural order of things.

Family is where new life is born—life conceived with the love, joy, and rapture that attends the sexual union between a man and a woman who are wholeheartedly committed to one another and who delight in living with and loving each other. This is a gift from God and tells us something about the great delight and love with which He created all life in the beginning.

That new life needs to be protected—nurtured and cared for. In a family, everyone is blessed as everyone's needs are met. Husbands serve the needs of their wives. Wives serve the needs of their husbands. Together, parents serve the needs of their children. Our word *family* is even rooted in servanthood. It comes from the root word *famulus*, which means "servant."

But what makes family the building block of society? Let's trace its far-reaching effects. Families live in homes or apartments. A cluster of such dwellings in a given area composes a block. A cluster of blocks composes a neighborhood. A cluster of neighborhoods comprises a community—a town or a city. A cluster of towns and cities comprises a county. A cluster of counties comprises a state. A cluster of states comprises a nation.

So what makes any particular nation a good nation? What makes for a good state, a good county, or a good neighborhood? The answer is simple: good families. From good families come people who understand the importance of living together in unity and peace, who relate to others with respect and kindness.

The moral quality of every individual human being who walks out the front door to interact with every other human being determines the quality and destiny of our neighborhoods, towns, states, and nation. And the quality of every individual is determined by the quality of the home each one came from. Thus, as the Pope said, as go our homes, so goes our nation—and even the world. Our mutual security, our peace, our prosperity all depend on each one of us being the right kind of people, which, in turn, depends on how we are raised.

Truly good human beings—decent, honest, hardworking, and responsible—are not born, they are made. Each baby has the potential to make a big difference in the world, for better or worse. So, parents take on an awesome responsibility when they bring a child into the world. Within the family, children first learn the important lessons of life. They learn right from wrong. They learn how to socialize, how to get along with others. They learn, by experience, how to successfully live with others. By living within a family, children learn what it takes to be a successful mother and a successful father as they watch their parents model loving sacrifice for them year after year. We learn how husbands and wives ought to treat one another, how parents should treat their children, and how children should properly respond to the authority and guidance of their parents. Within a family where vows and commitments are taken seriously, children first learn the importance of keeping their word, especially where someone else's heart and well-being is involved.

We parents are responsible, not just for laying the foundation of our children's lives, but also for impacting society through their lives. True, our children are free moral agents who will, in time, become responsible for themselves. How they turn out, however, has a great deal to do with how well we did our jobs.

The problem today is that more people are growing up absolutely clueless as to why family is an ideal. And clueless as to how to go about having a solid and stable family of their own. Children are increasingly growing up in homes that have been, in the midst of bitterness and hatefulness, smashed to smithereens. Multiple stepmoms, stepdads, and steprelatives wander through their lives, impacting them in all sorts of ways. And the result? An entire generation utterly unequipped to lead normal family lives. They have never known what a normal family is!

The bottom line is that parents cannot impart truth they don't know, principles they don't live by, or wisdom they don't possess. Parents are the leaders in the home; but looking at the degree of "expertise" in today's average parent, I'm reminded of what Jesus said concerning leaders who were not up to the task: "If a blind man leads a blind man, both will fall into a pit" (Matthew 15:14).

Children are falling into pits everywhere we turn—pits of depression, rage, and suicide, pits so hard to climb out of.

Detonation of the Nuclear Family

I have collected some highlights, or perhaps lowlights, from Dr. Laura's programs broadcast in 1996, 1997, and 1998. To underscore the tragic nature of the problems, I have deleted Dr. Laura's comments and focused only on the callers' stories. Let's first consider the following divorce scenarios.

Caller: Well, I'm supposed to get married in September. I'm fifty-two, she's forty-eight, and it will be the fourth marriage for each of us. . . . I married one woman twice to protect the kids because she was alcoholic and abusive. She divorced three times because one husband beat her, one was a drunk, and the other one was a nitwit . . .

Caller: I am divorced, and my husband and I separated when I was six months pregnant because he had a girl-friend . . .

Caller: I'm planning on getting married this July. I've planned on not asking my dad to escort me down the aisle because he has not been a father to me. My parents have been divorced now for about eleven years; and during the past eleven years and the five years prior to that, my father was having extramarital affairs, very physically abusive and verbally abusive . . . to my older sister and I. . . . He would beat us. . . . But that was so minute compared to the emotional abuse . . .

Caller: To start off, I'm a thirty-seven-year-old single father of my son . . . his mother had a yearlong affair and left with someone else . . . though they haven't married. For about a year and a half now, we have shared custody of our son, so we both continue our relationship with him. . . . My boy lives with her half the time. She has him Mondays and Tuesdays and I have him Wednesdays and Thursdays, and we alternate weekends. My problem, Dr. Laura, is I've been dating a woman for about eight months now (who has two stepchildren from a previous marriage), and she wants to get married and have children with me . . .

Caller: My husband and I are raising my eight-year-old nephew. His mother called us about two and a half years ago, and he at the time, of course, was five and a half, and she said that we either needed to take him or she was going to have to put him in an institution. . . . She is not a candidate for mother of the year award. His dad keeps in touch maybe once a year, but he's never acknowledged paternity and never taken responsibility. Basically, he is a big playmate . . .

Caller: Well, just to give you a little background here . . . I got married when I was eighteen years old. I'm now forty-five. I married a twenty-seven-year-old divorced man who had custody of his four children, whom we raised. Their mother was just not into her kids. And we've had three of our own. The boy is the oldest and has been married twice. He has just, as a matter of fact, been released from prison. Anyway, my question for you is this. My husband and I have been married for almost twenty-seven years. He's always had a lot of drinking problems. Like you, I don't believe in alcoholism . . . anyway, a couple of months ago, I caught him with another woman . . .

Caller: My moral dilemma today is I've recently been divorced, and I have four beautiful children who I absolutely love . . . we wanted four children. Anyway, Mother and Father just couldn't see eye-to-eye on several things.

We tried our best . . . obviously not enough, so we got divorced—which was wrong. We should have tried to work it out. The kids are ages two to ten years old. The problem I have is . . . uh . . . she met somebody, and she was going to get married—which is OK—and then I found somebody also. I had somebody move in with me. The moral dilemma I have is, uh . . . I don't want to set a bad example for my children . . .

The heartbreak continues in the following shack-up scenarios.

Caller: OK . . . I've read your book and moved out from my last boyfriend. But I have another boyfriend now whom I've been living with for four months. I met him five months ago. So anyway, I came home from work on Saturday about 7:30, and he was all drunk . . . and I don't know what to do about it . . .

Caller: I guess I'm having a dilemma with my ex-common-law spouse. We were never married, but we were together for six years, in which space of time we had three children together. I was in love with him. I have a one-year-old boy, my second one. That's my youngest. My second is two and a half. She'll be three in February, three in a month. And my oldest is five. We're not together now, but we are trying to work things out. The problem is . . . he ended up with this girl, but he was screwing around before then even . . . and he hangs out at the bar and drinks constantly . . .

Caller: My problem is, I'm twenty-seven. I live with a twenty-year-old girl who has a five-year-old daughter. I have no children of my own. She was fifteen when she gave birth; and they got married and he left her two weeks after the baby was born. He decided that was not what he wanted, and he's twenty-seven also. So he was twenty-two when he got her pregnant at fifteen . . . OK. We've been shacking up for a year and a half. I wanted to marry her, but awhile back we found out my girl-friend's mother's boyfriend had been molesting my girl-friend's daughter . . .

Caller: My situation is, I have a boyfriend. I'm twenty-five and he's twenty-three. And we have a two-year-old daughter. We've been seeing each other since high school, and started living together after high school. Well, about two months ago, he came home and told me that he had cheated . . . he had slept with somebody . . . I guess he told me out of guilt. So I told him to leave, but it was really hard on our daughter not to have him there. I know we should have gotten married, but now I'm not sure I want to marry this person . . .

Finally, reflect on the pain in the following unwed mother scenarios.

Caller: Well, I'm divorced. I have two children, twelve and five, and last fall I did something stupid. I was dating this guy and ended up having sex with him and getting preg-nant. Now I'm about seven months along, and it's going to be twins . . . and the father took off when I told him I was pregnant . . . won't have anything to do with me . . .

Caller: Oh, gosh, where to begin . . . OK. I have a four-and-a-half-year-old daughter who I had with a guy that I dated for two months. He wanted nothing to do with it, wanted me to abort. I refused . . . I had a pretty lousy childhood with a single mom that was with guy after guy. . . . Now I'm facing another pregnancy, unmarried, and with another guy that doesn't want to be here. I completely realize all my mistakes, and I want to take responsibility for them, but I'm not sure which responsibility to take. I don't want to have another child with-out a dad . . . I don't want the financial struggles, but I'm selfish too, I don't want another baby right now . . .

Caller: OK. I have a question for you. I am a single mom of two. I was previously married, but the second one is six months old and has a different daddy. I'm not currently in a relationship with him. He chose, during my sixth month of pregnancy, to take a job in a different state . . .

Caller: OK. I guess I should get right to the point here. I have a two-and-a-half-year-old son. I'm twenty-one. I'm a single mom. My son's dad, his name is Mark, he is in and out of my son's life all the time. He's a dad at his convenience. Well, he's just had another baby, well, supposedly his son, with another woman. What should I do with the relationship as far as my son and his dad go? . . .

Sadly, these scenarios are as heartwrenching as they are common. The children will likely never learn what true love and family are all about. How will they be taught right from wrong? Their parents don't know it. How will they learn about commitment and respect? The parents don't have it. How will they become conscientious and loving parents? Their parents don't know how to be. The odds are against children raised like this ever being prepared to take their place in society as mature, responsible adults.

The most sobering thought, however, is the exponential increase that results when children from these types of unions hook up with their own recreational sex partners and produce even more kids they can't care for properly. And their kids will, in turn, grow up to perpetuate the cycle of neglect and poverty of character.

How inexpressibly sad that so many of these babies, who have such potential for goodness and productivity, are destined for failure because of whom they will be raised by.

A Lesson from (Not *for*) the Birds

Is it any wonder that Mother Laura has said, "We've lost the consciousness that children are the most important thing once we've obligated ourselves by having them."

In a January 1996 article in her *Go Take on the Day* newsletter, Dr. Laura asked, "Whatever happened to the nesting instinct?" She went on to ruminate about a conversation she'd had with a thirty-year-old woman who was actually proud that she wasn't living with her baby's father. This woman was pleased that they had done it "the nineties way"—intentionally conceiving their child out of wedlock. Dr. Laura is not shy about criticizing the famous Hollywood stars who have helped popularize this trend. Marginalizing the importance of fathers has hurt children more than they will ever know.

What was the moral dilemma this "nineties mother" was having? The dad, who saw his child on weekends, now wanted him to stay overnight on the weekends, and she didn't want to allow it. Her rationale? She "deserved" her son more than he did.

What kind of family philosophy is that? What kind of environment, what kind of life is that for a child? Children were meant to walk down the street hand in hand between Mom and Dad. Together. Not apart. Remember what God made us for? Life in loving union. To be a blessing to each other and help each other be a blessing to everyone else.

Dr. Laura pointed out what should have been obvious: Children need to be parented by both a mom *and* a dad, in one nest, together. Tragically, far too many parents think only of what's handy or helpful for them, not their child.

Take the woman who boasted about how fair she and her ex were being with their child. Why, they had managed to "split the child" fifty/fifty every couple of days throughout the week. She sounded so proud of herself, so happy about it all, that Dr. Laura had to say something. She asked abruptly, "How would *you* like to live like that?"

"What?" asked the caller in surprise.

"How would you like to live like that? You know, get your blankie, your bear, all your stuff, and go live in one house for a couple of days and get used to one routine. Then pack up everything and go to another house and adapt to another different routine. Then go back and do it all over again a couple of days later. Back and forth. Back and forth. Back and forth. I mean would you *personally* want to live a life like that?"

After a long, long pause, the woman haltingly said, "Uh . . . no. I guess I wouldn't."

"Thank you!" Dr. Laura replied.

How many parents would not want to live the life they've given their own kids?

Dr. Laura concluded her article by observing, "The ultimate great mother is one who makes a nest before making babies. Birds do it as a matter of course. Why is it that human women have so much trouble with the concept?"

Kathleen Flanagan, a conservative political/educational activist in California's Bay Area, and a friend of mine, sent the following letter to me last year. It dovetails well with Dr. Laura's comments.

> Hi, Ray,
>
> It's just overwhelming, isn't it, when one considers the degeneration of our society? I've been spending an inordinate amount of time lately watching a pair of mourning doves who have made their home in my hanging basket of a now very, very dead fuschia, right outside my front door. Of course, like most gifts in life, it's been a real learning experience. The parents dote on these babies, never leaving them alone for a moment. It's obvious these parents know that parenthood is responsibility, sacrifice, love, and devotion.
>
> No, they don't have the best nest in the neighborhood—mourning doves build extremely shabby nests! But the parents mate for life, and either Mom or Dad dove is tending to the babies at all times. Last Sunday I spent nearly three hours watching the parents let the little fledglings know it was time to leave the nest. They literally pushed Baby Dove #2 right out into the world! Although Baby Dove was forced to spend the night hud-

dling beneath a large bush in my atrium entryway, Mom and Dad were watching over him all night until he finally earned his "wings."

I think, Ray, that today's parents could have used a course in bird-watching rather than sex education. They would have learned a heck of a lot more about love and responsibility than they have from all the . . . education they've received.

And they would have learned that the fine, new, bigger house means nothing to a child who has been dropped in a day care center to be raised by someone else. Even "birdbrains" know it doesn't take a village to raise a child; it takes two, loving parents.

| **Storm Clouds** | A listener sent the following list to Dr. Laura, comparing what teachers considered the biggest problems to be in 1940 and 1990:

1940	1990
Talking out of turn	Drug abuse
Chewing gum	Alcohol abuse
Making noise	Pregnancy
Running in the halls	Suicide
Cutting in line	Rape
Dress code infractions	Robbery
Littering	Assault

Incredible! In 1940 the problems were immaturity, natural carelessness, and inattention to detail common to young people. We can safely shrug off these behaviors—"Oh well, kids will be kids"—because we know kids outgrow them.

But how on earth are we supposed to respond to the second list? Will kids outgrow these? We can't exactly dismiss these like the others.

"Oh well, kids will be criminals!"

131

"Oh well, kids will be callous, cold-blooded, and ruthless!"

"Oh well, kids will be drug addicts and alcoholics!"

"Oh well, kids will be discovering that life truly isn't worth
living."

"Oh well, kids will be promiscuous!"

Actually, adults have been saying this last line for years. Educational leaders, politicians, and activists have told kids this for so long
to justify ridiculous sex education programs and condom distribution
that we shouldn't be surprised that the kids now accept it as
inevitable. We shouldn't be surprised that two out of three high
schoolers are sexually active and that the average age of their first sexual encounter has dropped to under sixteen years of age. At the last
World Conference on AIDS at the United Nations, a well-known
Hollywood star "astutely" recommended that parents who truly
loved their kids keep a "nonjudgmental box" of at least two hundred
condoms around the house. Hey! "Kids will be kids."

This is known as a decline in civilization.

The year before my family and I came to Hesperia, my kids
spent one year at their parents' high school. When my wife and I set
foot on campus twenty years after we had been students there, it
took our breath away. All the vending machines that used to sit out
in the open were now in huge iron cages to prevent vandalism and
theft. Ditto for all the banks of lockers that once upon a time no one
bothered. The trash was ankle-deep everywhere. Good kids, nice
kids, were hard to spot. My own kids stuck out like sore thumbs.
Decent students used to be the rule, and the violent, thuggish delinquents were the exception. Now it's the other way around. When I
was in high school, we didn't need a security detail to check students
in the hallway, fences around the perimeter of the school with
manned security checkpoints at locked gates, or full-time sheriff's
deputies on staff who had their own squad car parking space next to
the principal's. The school we had known and loved—in just one
generation—now looked and felt more like a stalag.

Drops of Rain If teachers were to update that list of the biggest problems faced in schools, they would have to add at least two more items: mass murder and just plain evil.

October 10, 1998, a fourteen- and fifteen-year-old brother and sister poisoned their own mother's iced tea because their parents had grounded them the previous week.

November 12, 1996, Amy Grossberg and Brian Petersen delivered their baby boy in a motel room, murdered him, and dumped him into a trash bin.

May 21, 1998, in Springfield, Oregon, Kipland Kinkel, age fourteen, killed four people, two of whom were his parents. He then proceeded to injure twenty-two others in a school shooting.

In Jonesboro, Arkansas, a thirteen-year-old and an eleven-year-old allegedly killed four young girls, one teacher, and wounded ten others.

A fourteen-year-old in Redlands, California, left school a couple of years ago and returned with a sawed-off shotgun under his coat and shot a school official.

As I write this, hearing dates are being set for two of the three boys who are accused of plotting to take over Burlington High School and kill certain students and staff in Racine, Wisconsin.

How could this happen? we ask. How did it come to be this way? Where is it safe anymore? What's gotten into kids nowadays?

Raindrops in a Hurricane Here is Dr. Laura's answer to this big question, in what I think is one of the finest monologues she's ever delivered.

I have something I think is very important to say. This seems kind of stupid because, frankly, every time I open my mouth I'm trying to be important. But I think you better listen up. It's one of those situations where, when you look at a unique event, say, one raindrop falling from the heavens, you say, "It's a unique experience."

But if you stand back and see that there are 40 million scrillion raindrops falling from the heavens with a big wind behind them, you have a whole different perspective. When you stand back and look at the whole of it, you see you're in a hurricane and the top of your house just went. So perspective is everything. If you stand back and look at each event, define it, and put it away, you can feel very safe—but you're not. You better stand back and see that it's one raindrop in a hurricane.

On my way to work today, I heard about the student in the public high school in Oregon who killed his parents and his sister, somebody else at school, and a score or two of other children are seriously hurt. If you look at each one of these events, kids doing drive-by shootings . . . just take one event in the newspaper, on one day, you think, "Bad kid. Shooting each other in schools. Isolated event. Bad kid." Kids committing suicide at rates unknown in modern times . . . kids having babies at eleven and twelve and thirteen and fourteen and fifteen and sixteen, and killing them. Wrapping them up in a towel and burying them in the earth, or flushing them down a toilet. It's an isolated event. The kids on drugs and alcohol at levels I never heard of when I was a kid. If somebody sneaked a beer that was a big deal.

If you listen to this program at all, you can tell that there are very few parents out there who feel any sense of authority with their children. The children rule. So if you stand back and look at all of these things, not as an isolated raindrop, you see an apocalypse. I am really dead serious about this, and it would seem lately, more and more, *dead* is the operative word.

I perceive this as the ultimate in backlash and revenge of the children brought up by a generation who invented a whole new way of life. New and improved way of life. And these are the improvements. Commitment is temporary. We've redefined it. There are even books out called *A Good Divorce*. We've got people shacking up, making babies, moving on, . . . not seeing their kids, and moving away. Judges saying, "Not a problem. You want to move your kids away from their dad? Honey-babe, you deserve to be happy. Screw the kid." Got women living with guys they're not married to who are molesting their children, at much higher rates than marital situations by far. We have day care. That's new and improved. Women have the right to abandon their children, and their children will be happy about it as long as the mommies are happy. Whose moronic idea is that? Abortion is commonplace. You get pregnant, you don't want it, you suck it into a sink. No problem. It's not a person.

You don't think all this cultivates a complete irreverence for life? How can children feel important when they're not? Whether you stay married. Whether you are married. It's all unimportant. The children don't matter. It's your own happiness that counts. So we have chaos in the home. We have, therefore, chaos in society. My children are not safe from your children anymore. These are not isolated raindrops. . . .

The best new-and-improved idea in our society is to remove God as an issue in the family, so that all holidays we have now have magazines and news articles extolling the virtues of interfaith-less marriages. . . . We've more and more become unwilling to study, to pray, to observe our religion because, you know why? It's time-consuming and annoying, and it's not really necessary anyway. The most important thing is my fulfillment. So our generation provided this chaos, this lack of home, lack of parents, lack of family, lack of stability, lack of reverence for life, lack of God. And now we have a big hurricane.

When I was on "Meet the Press" (after another time some kids had killed at other schools), I don't think anybody heard me clearly. Maybe I said it too tactfully, so I'm going to be a little less tactful now. This is a lab experiment that failed. We've created a national "Lord of the Flies." Kids have no respect for life. They know they're not important. They don't see any purpose. They don't see any security. They don't ultimately see any love, because we have no time and no interest in anything but acquisition. That's what's important. Character, fidelity, stability, the preciousness of life, God—these are not relevant as long as the economy is OK. Isn't that indicative of "we don't care"? I'm not the slightest bit surprised, although I am beyond myself in grief for the parents who are losing children this way. I mean, I can't imagine the pain of sending your kid to school and having this happen. Even the threat of it. But our kids are going to continue to do drive-bys; mass murder in school; to make babies, abandon, abuse, and kill them; be on drugs and alcohol and scare the fire out of you and everybody else and each other because we taught them that they don't matter and nothing else does. This is the revenge for our new order. You still want to argue with me?

Hurricane Season Is Here No argument here. The hurricane season is just beginning.

In February 1996, Robert L. Maginnis, a policy analyst with the Family Research Council, a Washington, D.C.–based research and advocacy organization, wrote a thoroughly documented report titled "Unprecedented Surge in Future Youth Crime."[3] The basic premise of the report is that, in spite of the decrease in some of the national major crime statistics, we must not be lulled into a false sense of security. The reason for his contention? The continuing escalation of serious crimes by youth and the family-related circumstances that are producing a growing number of that kind of youth. Here are just a few of the statistical highlights:

> Violent crime involving young people, both as perpetrators and victims, is on the rise. "The number of juveniles arrested for

weapons offenses has more than doubled over the past decade," noted FBI Director Louis Freeh.

On a typical day in 1994, nine teenagers in the U.S. were murdered and thirteen teenagers committed a murder.

In 1965, 23-year-olds were arrested more often for murder than any other age group, and their rate was 33 per 100,000 23-year-olds. In 1992, 18-year-olds were arrested more often for murder, and their rate was 97 per 100,000 18-year-olds. That's a 467 percent increase in murder arrests for 18-year-olds. The trend is toward younger offenders and higher arrest rates.

According to Attorney General Janet Reno, the problem of children killing will only worsen because demographics show the key at-risk population, fourteen- to seventeen-year-olds, will increase significantly in years to come.

Mr. Maginnis points out that social scientists have demonstrated that certain domestic conditions are closely tied to juvenile violence. Among them:

Parental absence increases a child's likelihood of future criminal behavior.

As out-of-wedlock birth has risen, so has the crime rate. Forty-three percent of all inmates grew up in a single-parent household.

Cato Institute Chairman William Niskanen said, "A one-percentage-point increase in births to single mothers appears to increase the violent crime rate about 1.7 percent."

A 1990 study by June O'Neill, a professor with Baruch College of the City University of New York, shows that men from single-parent families are twice as likely to commit crimes as men from two-parent families.

Robert Sampson, professor of sociology at the University of Chicago, notes that it is harder for single-parent families to achieve the "informal social controls" that limit both crime and victimization within a community. "There are higher crime rates in places where communities are not characterized by strong families," Sampson said.

Mr. Maginnis also quotes a Justice Department study. It concludes that parental supervision, attachment to family, and consistency of discipline are the most important barriers to delinquency and drug abuse.

Reaping the Whirlwind

In confronting Israel's apostasy in his day, the prophet Hosea pointed out that the nation had let the commandments of God become something alien, unknown to them. Having forgotten God and His Law, they became preoccupied with the material side of life and were busy building their palaces. Too busy to worry about something as trivial as law and morality. Hey, "the economy was doing good." Ever heard that one before?

But it was in this context that Hosea said,

> They sow the wind
>   and reap the whirlwind. (Hosea 8:7)

There is just no getting around the "law of harvest." If you plant corn, you get corn. If you plant potatoes, you get potatoes. If you plant chaos, you will reap chaos. As the Apostle Paul reiterated, "Do not be deceived: God cannot be mocked. A man"—or a nation, for that matter—"reaps what he sows" (Galatians 6:7).

We have scrapped God, undermined the family, and now our society has grown dangerous. We will also reap our own whirlwind, a storm whose clouds we ourselves have seeded and whose torrential downpour has really only just begun.

So Where Do We Go from Here?

If Dr. Laura should decide to retire and turn off her microphone tomorrow, it could be rightfully argued that her greatest legacy will have been restoring the supreme importance that the nuclear family bears to a healthy society. She has championed the traditional two-parent home and the surpassing importance of children.

"For the children" is not an empty slogan she bandies about for personal gain. She really cares about them and runs a foundation dedicated to preventing child abuse, promoting adoption, and more, to prove it. She reveals clearly the relationship between the destruction of the traditional family and the problems facing—and vanquishing—so many of our young people. She establishes convincingly the link between abolishing the Judeo-Christian ethic and the current immoral and violent state of the union.

Kids can't fix this. It's up to every responsible adult in the country. We have to get our heads screwed back on straight and begin living the right values and priorities.

Dr. Laura's "family bandwagon" is worth jumping on. She's out making a real dent in evil by prescribing God and scriptural ethics to "everybody and their mother." We would all do well to make it as large a priority as she has.

"I Am My Kid's Mom"

> "I am my kid's mom" because I remind myself all the time, every day, of what my primary responsibility is.
>
> *Dr. Laura*

A Simple Priority | "I Am My Kid's Mom" has become part of our national vocabulary, thanks to Dr. Laura's mission to remind us of the importance of mothers actually mothering their own children. Amazingly, though, many people haven't a clue as to what her trademark introduction means. Her critics often attack her for what they believe is her hypocrisy in saying it, since she says it on the air as a working mother.

Out of all the times she has patiently offered her perspective on this, I think the following monologue is one of the most complete explanations she has ever made. It answers her critics and, at the same time, elaborates on the heart of her motto—being there for our kids.

I was interviewed on a station the other day, in the East, and I got the same old question: "How can you talk about working mothers when, number one, you are one;

and number two, you're on the lecture circuit?"

Coupla things. One, I have to be in this chair from eleven to two Monday through Friday. Saturday is the Sabbath, I ain't goin' nowhere. When am I on this lecture circuit? I'm dying to know when I'm on this lecture circuit. And if I'm on this lecture circuit, where's the money? I want to know where the money is! The standing joke in our offices downstairs is, "Don't bother to ask her; she'll say no." So they have special tactics now they use to try to get me to do something. "*No!* That's more than a half an hour from my house, and my kid can't come, so it's not happening!" Now there are some obligations a couple of times a year I have to do, so I do it. Or if it's something for charity, I do that. Got Dad at home. If I'm gone for one day, this is not a problem. Normally, I'm home when my kid is home.

This is just hysterical. The assumption nowadays is that if you achieve a certain level of success, that you had to have sacrificed something else. The answer is no. All you have to decide is which is more important. For me, it's family. You know how people have on their license plate frames, "I'd rather be skiing?" I'd rather be home . . . I'm a homebody! Yes, the program is doing well, and that's a fact. But it's three hours a day, and after that, I'm outta here—to everyone's dismay. They're trying to get me to sign something, read something, do something . . . "*Goin' home*" . . . (laughing). I could be doing all kinds of other things if I sacrificed family. . . . The truth is, you make decisions and you have to have priorities. . . .

Now, we have ways in which we can have kids and not put any energy into it (it's called day care). You can put those things on your computer where you can watch the little boogers sit there and whine, and you can see that they haven't been eaten by a pit bull. They have telephone lines they can call now when they are feeling sad or need help on their homework. We have ways of having kids and doing nothing with, for, or about them . . . except come home eventually and think it's cute when we tuck them in. If we put that much energy into our work, we'd have our rear ends fired within three days! But our children can't fire us—till, of course, we're elderly.

In referring to mothers working outside the home, neither I nor Dr. Laura contend that there is anything wrong with the wife being an integral part of the home's economy. When we looked at the worthy woman in Proverbs 31, we saw clearly that the ideal wife and mother from God's perspective contributed to the financial well-being of her family:

> She considers a field and buys it;
>   out of her earnings she plants a vineyard.
> She sets about her work vigorously;
>   her arms are strong for her tasks.
> She sees that her trading is profitable,
>   and her lamp does not go out at night. . . .
> She makes linen garments and sells them,
>   and supplies the merchants with sashes. (vv. 16–18, 24)

Most cultures throughout history, including America's, have had agrarian economies, and the home was the center of that. Women have always worked just as hard as men to provide for their families. Only in modern times has the center of commerce moved away from the home so that we "go off to work" and "come home to rest." And most folks (like folks always) still need more than the income one person can provide.

But when it's time to raise the kids, it's time to raise the kids! If a woman wishes to have a career, by all means go for it! Just don't have any kids while you're at it. If you are going to have them, then give them the nest—the time and attention they deserve. *The kind you would want for yourself if you were a baby again.* No one can do for your child what you can.

The False Promise of Day Care

Dr. Laura's intention in introducing herself as her kid's mom is to emphasize the priority her son has in her life. Her job as a mother comes first, because raising Deryk is her most important responsibility. Raising their children is the most significant thing mothers can do.

Thanks to my wife's investment and devotion, we have a wonderful family. We're not rich monetarily. We're not famous as the world counts fame. We're not perfect by anybody's standards. But not a day goes by that we are not supremely thankful for the kind of hearth and home we have. Strong relationships. Open communication. Honesty. Trust. A close and intimate warmth. A common faith. None of it would have been possible, to the extent we have and enjoy it, without her.

Our children were all nurtured by their mother in a way no one else could have done. They were cared for with a level and quality of attention no one else would have given. Loved with a tenderness and intensity no one else could have felt. Protected with a fierceness no one else could have summoned.

The emotional support, the security and peace, and the sheer dependability that my wife provided in our children's crucial first years gave each of them a foundation of health and well-being. Every child deserves to have this start. And none can possibly receive this in private or federally funded day care—no matter what anybody in Washington says about it. No matter what "studies" are conducted by the likes of the University of Massachusetts at Amherst. Their conclusion was: "Mothers who work outside the home during the first three years of their children's lives do not harm their youngster's behavior, mental development, or self-esteem."[1]

Kathleen Parker responded to this study in *The Orlando Sentinel.* Among other things, she said, "Phooey!" A fitting word, judging from the following letter a listener, and ex-child care worker now turned "her kid's mom," wrote to Dr. Laura.

I'm writing because I would like to lend my voice of support to your wake-up call to moms everywhere concern-

144

ing the importance of being their kids' mom. Maybe the following will help those still on the fence, those still at least partially believing that they are making a justified choice to work outside of the house and put the kids in day care.

I worked in a day care environment for three years, both as an instructor and as a center director. With an undergraduate degree from a four-year college and graduate work in child psychology, I was one of the more educated and well-read people in the centers. Moreover, I love kids, I always have. I love tying shoes, reading stories, wiping noses, wiping tears, laughing at not-so-funny jokes. I thought at the time that I was a great caregiver. With two or three of the children, I formed very tight bonds and continued to stay in contact with the families, some up to five years later. In my mind, I loved those kids as my own.

Now on to reality. I gave birth eight-and-a-half months ago to a beautiful baby girl, and because of my husband's willingness to work harder and longer hours than the ideal forty-hour work week, I get to stay home and truly be her mommy. OK, this is where I would want all of those working moms to truly listen. The experience of being Sarah's mom has taught me that I never loved those other kids as my own. No matter what I thought or how caring and loving I was, no one except for my husband could ever love and care for Sarah the way I do. I don't care if you think that you have the ideal person tending to your child's needs while you work—you don't! Because you are that ideal person. Nothing is the same without that unique and invaluable love you provide to your own child. Could somebody else wipe Sarah's nose? Yes. Could somebody else teach her to say *up* and *puppy?* Sure. But would anybody besides her parents lay down life, limb, and soul for any and all reasons to protect her? No.

I will say it again. I thought I loved the children at the center as my own, but I did not. I thought I was offering what their parents could have offered—I did not. I thought they were receiving the maximum in caring and nurturing; they were not.

What this educated, experienced, and wise woman had learned, quite simply, is that there is no substitute for a mother. Absolutely, positively none. In fact, if there is one truly indispensable job in all the world, it is mothering.

I Am My Kid's Soldier?

My daughter Jessica and I love to watch movies together. One evening, back when she was fourteen, we sat down to watch *Courage Under Fire*, with Meg Ryan and Denzel Washington. Ryan's character, who had died before the story began, had wanted to be a pilot more than anything—including a mother. Denzel Washington was the military investigator trying to understand the circumstances surrounding the crash that resulted in Ryan's death. As he interviewed the survivors one by one, differing accounts emerged that smacked of a cover-up. When all was said and done, Meg Ryan was the hero. At the end, when Washington laid the Medal of Honor on her tombstone, stood back, and saluted, our popcorn really started getting soggy.

A subplot running through the movie involved Ryan's little daughter, whom she had to leave with Grandma and Grandpa when she deployed overseas. It seemed to me that this part of the film was saying, "I'm a woman going off to do a man's job as well as any man, and I sure love you, Sweetheart. And I know you love me, but duty calls and someone's got to do this. So I want you to understand why I'm doing what I'm doing, and I want you to be proud of me, because I'm sure proud of you. And you be a good little girl for Grandma and Grandpa now, and I won't ever forget you, and please don't ever forget me." Some of this was set down in a letter she had left with the grandparents in the unfortunate event of her demise.

When Jessica and I had finished blowing our noses, I asked her, "Honey, do you want to know what the single biggest problem with this movie is?" When she finished guessing, and she picked up on the child being orphaned, I told her that it was the message that mothers and their children are unimportant—or at least less important than flying and fighting. As a mother to her child, Ryan was indispensable, irreplaceable. No other soul on earth could be fully to her child what she was. As a mother she was absolutely unique. And she abandoned that position because she wanted to be a pilot. A position where she was dispensable, replaceable. You can always build more helicopters and train people to fly them, but children have only one mother.

Our conversation that evening was remarkably similar to the one Dr. Laura had with this particular caller:

Dr. Laura: Hi, welcome to the show.

Caller: Hi, Dr. Laura. Well, I'll try to get right to the point. I'm a member of the National Guard, and I've been informed that my unit is deploying to Europe in support of the Bosnia peace mission. . . . My moral dilemma right now is that I have a ten-week-old baby . . .

Dr. Laura: Tell me you're a married lady.

Caller: I'm married! I'm twenty-seven years old, and my husband is the best father on the face of the planet. Um . . . the dilemma I'm facing is that my commander has presented me with an option I'm . . . I'm not sure is ethical in terms of trying to get out of the deployment . . .

Dr. Laura: What do you mean "not ethical"?

Caller: Well . . . because I've enlisted in the National Guard. The military has been a big, important part of my life for about ten years now, and I kind of feel like if I'm not willing to deploy, then I shouldn't be in the National Guard.

Dr. Laura: Well, maybe that's so, but there are tasks that National Guard people can also do right here . . . and . . . I don't think women with babies should be in the military at all, period! At any level of any kind of military for this very reason: the babies need the mommy. So, it's sort of an interesting discussion we're going to have here now, because I'm sure there are tasks you can do here while you do the parenting that such a young baby needs.

Caller: Well, that's what my commander was saying, though it's not guaranteed that I'd be allowed to . . .

Dr. Laura: I understand that, but I don't think mothers should be away from their babies, period. I don't think they should be in the military . . .

Caller: So do you think that women shouldn't be in the military? I mean . . .

Dr. Laura: Well, maybe if they take their ovaries out and throw them on the floor, or they're postmenopausal or something. But not when they're making babies! I don't devalue family, and I don't devalue babies. I think that's infinitely more important than you shooting a gun. Sorry! We got enough guys to do that!

The Importance of Fathers

Speaking of guys, Dr. Laura continually emphasizes the importance of fathers within the family. One of the most destructive consequences of feminism is not just the trivializing of motherhood but the devaluing of fatherhood as well. Nothing makes Mother Laura madder than people who prattle on about how unnecessary fathers are:

> I am furious, I am furious, and I am furious! This was published Sunday, March 2, in *The Miami Herald*. And I love the way articles like this are published with no judgment, no commentary. But let me say something about shacking up, and they'll judge me all over the place. But listen to this, this isn't judged. Don't tell me there isn't a slant and a bias in the media. All you have to do is look at what's presented and what's judged.
>
> "In Fort Lauderdale and Miami, a support group for

single mothers." Now, we're not talking about your husband died here. We're talking about *we don't need no man!* Is that how they talk in Fort Lauderdale? I don't think so. They tout this motto: "Pregnancy by Any Means Necessary." They have a World Wide Web page devoted to sperm donors that features conversations about artificial insemination. Another offers a mother a sibling child registry so, you know, if we all use the same vial, we can check to see whose kids are related to whose, and we'll make sure they won't commit incest when they do it the old fashioned way—that is, actually have a relationship. These are women who, in my opinion, are incompetent to have a relationship. . . .

We all grew up thinking we would have a husband, a marriage, and then a family. At a certain point, you can't wait any longer. You have to give up that dream and have another dream. It's a readjustment, not a tragedy, and it's an increasing phenomenon. She got knocked up. I'm sorry, that's not what she says. She *got pregnant unexpectedly* while in a relationship with a man who made it clear he wanted no part of parenthood. She mulled over her choices. She decided her ovaries weren't getting any younger. Baby time. Now listen to this lie. "After much soul-searching and angst, others are making similar choices." Bull. After wallowing in your own self-pity and deciding what you want is more important than what a child needs, you make a similar choice. After discovering you don't know how to have a quality relationship with a man, you make the same choice.

Executive director of the sperm bank of California in Berkeley is another one with an idiotic idea. She says, "I think there is definitely a trend because, for a lot of women, the only thing missing in their lives is a kid." And what's going to be missing from the life of the kid? Or does anybody give a darn? And we have another idiot comment. You ready for this? This one comes from a man. It shows equal-opportunity stupidity. The director of the baby-making department at South Florida Institute for Reproductive Medicine in South Miami: "The desire for women to do this may not be new, but women are becoming more confident in themselves, and they are acting on an emerging sense of independence."

Now it's healthy for women not to be able to have a marital relationship, or not even to want one. It's actually an accomplishment. This sense of independence, making babies without fathers. It's now an accomplishment. If you don't think this is a bizarre and sickening distortion of femininity, feminism ideals, then I don't know what is. No dads. This is such a joke. . . . It's disgusting and despicable that there are women like this who intentionally obligate a child to no parent. It's despicable.

And that *The Miami Herald* could publish an article just stating the facts, ma'am, only the facts. Don't tell me they don't editorialize. I've read every article written about me, and there's editorializing all over the place. *How dare she?* And they'll put adjectives and adverbs, you know, to make it look like my espousing values is somehow bad or wrong or judgmental and overbearing. Yet when women can intentionally ensure no father for their children, there's not even an adjective in here. I think that is an immoral stance. If a woman wants it, it's OK. Your needs must be met. Doesn't matter who you mess over, including your own children.

Training up a Child

Historically, scripturally, and biologically, a child's best prospect for a happy and healthy start in life begins with parents who devote themselves to providing a stable, loving, and nurturing family life. Such was the case in Jesus' life. The Gospel of Luke tells us,

Jesus grew in wisdom and stature, and in favor with God and men. (Luke 2:52)

In only a few words, Luke has described Jesus' well-rounded upbringing. He grew in

wisdom—mental development;
stature—physical development;
favor with God—spiritual development;
favor with people—social development.

Tending to a child's nutritional, hygienic, and health needs should be obvious. What often gets overlooked, though, are the paramount areas of intellectual, spiritual, and social development. Let's take a look at each of these areas.

Intellectual Development

In recent years, every study I've read has disclosed the depressing reality that, although we spend more money on education—more dollars per kid—than any other industrialized nation in the world, we have consistently ranked at or near the bottom in literacy, math, and science. I guess the good news is that we have more teenagers than the rest of the world combined who know how to put condoms on bananas!

Seriously, kids who have a mom or dad around most of the time to supervise, who are made to do their homework, who are helped with their homework, will do well. But kids who have just graduated from day care into "latchkeydom" will, during the rest of their school career, sit home by themselves. What will they do with their time until their parents come home?

A. Study hard all by themselves.
B. Watch TV and videos.
C. Play Nintendo and computer games.
D. Surf pornographic Web sites.
E. Talk on the phone with their friends.
F. Rove the neighborhood in bands learning how to
   become juvenile delinquents.
G. Experiment with drugs, sex, and alcohol.
H. B through G.

You don't have to be a prophet to see what society will become when it's peopled with such untrained, undeveloped individuals.

Spiritual Development

Train a child in the way he should go,
and when he is old he will not turn from it.

(Proverbs 22:6)

Many children are not aware of their need for God because their parents are not demonstrating any awareness themselves. If parents never crack open a Bible, how will children see the benefits of Scripture study? How will they learn the value of worship if their parents go to church only at Easter and Christmas? If we would have our faith mean something to our children, it must first mean something to us. It's so important for parents to sincerely live out their faith in front of their children. Moses admonished:

Only be careful, and watch yourselves closely so that you do not forget the things your eyes have seen or let them slip from your heart as long as you live. Teach them to your children and to their children after them. Remember the day you stood before the Lord your God at Horeb, when he said to me, "Assemble the people before me to hear my words so that they may learn to revere me as long as they live in the land and may teach them to their children." (Deuteronomy 4:9-10)

In Ephesians 6:4, we have this simple counsel:

Fathers, do not exasperate your children; instead, bring them up in the training and instruction of the Lord.

Obviously, when both parents have a united spiritual front and the same worldview, they can more easily and effectively develop their children's spirituality. One of Dr. Laura's recurring themes is the importance of marrying a person of the same faith. Those starry-eyed young lovers, for whom differences in faith come dead last on the list of marital criteria, are almost always surprised by how important they become as they grow older. Dr. Laura speaks disparagingly of such mixed-faith marriages because it's just plain hard to pull a plow when you've got two horses going in different directions.

Social Development

Good social skills depend on teaching our children proper respect and regard for others. The best way to help them learn this is to show them that everybody is important. Unfortunately, judging by the atmospheres of our schools, parents haven't spent enough time on this.

I know a young twelve year old who goes to a public school where many of the kids seem to have no regard for anyone but themselves. They probably haven't had much spiritual instruction, from what their behavior indicates. Their conversations are marked by vulgar, foul language. The boys trash-talk, bully people, and make crude remarks about girls walking past them—"I'd do her! Wouldn't you like to do her?" These are sixth and seventh graders— eleven- to thirteen-year-olds swearing, menacing, and sexualizing themselves and others.

All of this points out how the drastic shortage of real "kid's moms and dads." But this situation cannot be blamed entirely on the break-down of the family or the gross lack of intellectual and spiritual train-ing. The modern god of television has to take part of the blame too.

Diode Deities and Empty Dinner Tables

Our society has elevated self-gratifi-cation through entertainment to an art form. Not because it has our best interests at heart, but because it makes a substantial profit for the peo-ple dispensing it. Daily we view more and more ways to cultivate a self-centered lifestyle. All of our electronic toys, and television in par-ticular, have contributed more to America's hedonism than probably anything else.

Now, I'm not declaring that entertainment is inherently evil. It's not, nor are its various media. But we have a knack for misusing things more than using them properly—for good. Many films and TV programs, as well as much music, has, in the last three decades, gone from a merely superficial, pop mentality to a downright evil and dangerous agenda. Disrespectful and hostile characters have become role models, and violent lyrics have indoctrinated legions of young people.

But it's not just the overtly bad TV that's the problem. It's the mindless excess of what many regard as wholesome. "Green Acres is the place to be," goes the song. It may be a nice place to visit, but we don't need to be *living* there! For all you parents out there who have used *Nickelodeon* and *TV Land* as your electronic nanny because of how harmless the good ole' shows were, guess what? Too much mindless froth is *not* a good thing! We need a little moderation here.

We have been trivializing ourselves into oblivion. With eyes and ears enlarged and brains atrophied, we have sacrificed ourselves and our children on the altar of name-brand electronics. Indiscriminate use of our toys has meant the decline of scholastic achievement, healthful exercise, good books, worship, high-quality family relationships, and all kinds of other constructive and meaningful activities.

We don't even eat together anymore.

About twelve or thirteen years ago, *The San Francisco Chronicle* ran a series of articles profiling trends in family life. One story had an accompanying photo of a young adolescent perched in front of his own television. His dinner was on a tray, and he was engrossed in one of his favorite programs. The article explained that his whole family looked forward to relaxing at dinnertime with their favorite television programs. The catch was, they each had different tastes. So every evening, the father, the mother, and the two kids got their own dinners, went to their own rooms, turned on their own TV sets, and watched their own programs by themselves. When asked how they liked this arrangement, they were all enthusiastic.

The statistics cited at the end of the article were dismal. Fewer than 50 percent of families had a traditional dinner hour together. Now, fast forward in time to Dr. Laura's observations today:

This was sent out by the Associated Press: "Something about eating meals with an adult in the family might help teenagers' psychological adjustment, a preliminary study suggests."

That's how far psychology has gone, that something so obvious as a family eating together has to be studied, and if there's anything good about it, it's only preliminary. Is this like reinventing the most obvious wheel? Then they took a survey of some teens, twelve to eighteen, and found that those who showed good signs of adjustment ate a meal with an adult in their family an average of five days a week versus three days for teens who don't show such good adjustment. You ready for the next statement? "But that doesn't prove that meals promote adjustment." This is so stupid I'm embarrassed to read it to you. "In fact, the higher number of meals reported by adjusted kids is probably just an indicator of something else that influences adjustment," said the author.

Now after I've called this stupid, I cannot possibly give you the author's name . . . this is so dumb. Duh! Maybe it's a family that gives a hoot, duh! Oh, dear. . . . "Nonetheless, the findings suggested it would be worth looking for something related to meals that promotes adjustment in teenagers," this researcher said. . . .

The person who sent this to me wrote in the margin, "You'd think it might be as simple as showing teens that the adult cares enough to eat with them." That's the most brilliant conclusion. However, it's only preliminary. Oh man, oh man, oh man, this psychobabble mentality is just bizarre. Next, you're going to find something about hugging a kid helps with their psychological adjustment. We don't know if it's just the smell of perfume or aftershave, and that's only preliminary. We'll work on this, it might be that if you take the time to hug them and they feel loved that they're better adjusted, but that's only one possible conclusion and it's preliminary. Thank heavens for popular psychology.

Next, she took on parenting magazines:

> Once a week . . . c'mon . . . once a week, eat dinner as a family. What? You mean to tell me we're living in a country where you have to tell people they should actually eat—break bread with—their spouse and their children? Huh?
>
> And I also remember when I read . . . it was all over the place, a recommendation from a psychiatrist back East. That you only need to spend fifteen minutes a day for adequate quality time with your children . . . fifteen minutes a day! So I challenge you folks. Try to have a relationship with anybody where you're only talking to each other for fifteen minutes a day. Let's see how long you date that person. Let's see how long you stay married. Let's see how close your children stay connected to you. Why would you want to believe that your kids only need you for fifteen minutes? I would have thought that if child psychiatrists had made these kinds of statements twenty years ago, that they would probably have been excoriated, humiliated, and drummed out of the corps. Now, it's scarfed up by parenting magazines, so we don't have to feel guilty that we are ignoring our children!

The Leaders We Deserve?

Dr. Laura's continual emphasis on family and character is a far more reasonable, and simple, solution than anything we are going to get from our current crop of government officials. Our society has increasingly relied on government to provide the answers and solutions to the hurricane we discussed in the last chapter. Begging your pardon, folks, but it is our politicians, in ever-increasing numbers, who have been seeding the clouds. Might as well put the fox in charge of guarding the henhouse! I would strongly suggest that every truly family-oriented person who has a streak of "old-fashioned" in him or her start paying attention to what our leaders are doing, not what they're saying.

Too many of our leaders, and we know who they are, have begun to use "the children" as nothing more than a hot button to press whenever they want to make the country feel that they really care. I've lost count how many times our President and Vice-President have used this as nothing more than an "image is everything" soundbite. On the campaign trail in 1992, Clinton made a speech where he said, "I want an America where family values live in our actions, not just in our speeches."[2] Judging from his own actions, he must have been talking about his own speeches.

This "for the children" administration is the same administration, of course, that promised us the most ethical administration in history. The same one that told us on the twenty-fifth anniversary of Roe v. Wade that, "Roe v. Wade [was] the landmark Supreme Court decision that affirmed every woman's right to choose whether and when to have a child, and in doing so, affirmed two of our nation's most deeply-held values, personal privacy and family responsibility."[3] *Abortion on demand equals family responsibility?*

Picture this. A country whose political leaders are increasingly distancing themselves from any kind of sincere, traditional faith. You know, the kind that says, "In God We Trust"—but get those Ten Commandments off that wall! Leaders who are rejecting traditional standards. Who are actively promoting abortion, the radical homosexual and feminist agendas, and putting into place all kinds of legislation that undermine the traditional family. Who are currently working hard at institutionalizing day care, actually touting that it can offer things to children they can't get at home. To top it all off, they are calling this the "bridge to the twenty-first century."

This is a bridge too far, and one I have no interest in crossing. We've already seen where that bridge is going to lead us. Why on earth would we have *any* confidence that the government is going to solve some of our biggest problems when it has been at the very root of them?

In Dr. Laura's first no-holds-barred monologue against the ethical mores of our current administration, she makes these chilling observations:

> This is a very serious problem . . . President Bill Clinton unzipping his fly, having Monica Lewinsky do him in the hallway, in the bathroom, in the Oval Office and then lying about it to a jury and whoever else. . . . I think if he had any character he'd walk away knowing how destructive he's been. For a year, this country has been torn up with this because of his lies and his bad behavior. Don't give me Linda Tripp, don't give me Kenneth Starr. If the man hadn't dropped his drawers time after time for a young intern, we wouldn't be here agonizing like this. . . . I have had enough of it. The part that really rankles, saddens, and upsets me is two-thirds of this country is going, "So what?" And do you know why you are doing that? It's because so many of you are screwing around on your spouses, you're all lying about stuff at work and at home, and you see yourself in the President . . . and you will not judge yourselves harshly.

Walter Williams, professor of economics at Virginia's George Mason University and syndicated columnist, points out in his column titled "What's Happened to Us?" that the public's response to all of the Clinton scandals is symptomatic of a problem "far more devastating than a president committing perjury and obstruction." He reminds us that our basic institutions survived presidential scandal before, such as when Warren Harding and Richard Nixon disgraced their office. But he notes this crucial difference: "This is the first time in our history we've had a president disgrace his office and receive widespread political and public support while doing so."[4]

It's time to lay aside our remote controls, quit relying on the "image is everything" method of political "canned-pains," and take a more active and informed part in our own political process. We actually need to investigate the legislative record and social agenda of these leaders who oppose traditional values and traditional family. Vote them out and vote people in who will take us back to the common sense and the Bible-based morality of the founding fathers and the Founding Father. Forget the Family 2000 program already being discussed by some in the context of social services for families. We need leaders with a family vision that will actually help restore the American home. The honesty, integrity, and faith of our citizenry has far more to do with the long-term viability of our country than Social Security or Medicare (not that those are unimportant).

We are running out of time. The above quotes (among many other things) would indicate that it is getting awfully late in the game for a comeback. The words of Edmund Burke, the English parliamentarian, are growing louder every day it seems: "All that is necessary for evil to triumph is for good men to do nothing."

Get busy.

Restoring Home Life . . . the Greatest Legacy

The Judeo-Christian Scriptures call us to real meaning and substance and can, therefore, help us restore a healthy home life. Consider the Apostle Paul's exhortation:

> So be very careful about the sort of lives you lead, like intelligent and not like senseless people. Make the best of the present time, for it is a wicked age. This is why you must not be thoughtless but must recognise what is the will of the Lord. (Ephesians 5:15-17, *New Jerusalem Bible*)

One way we can do this is to monitor more carefully what our kids take in. Paul gives us some helpful guidance on this in Philippians 4:8:

Finally, brothers, whatever is true, whatever is noble, whatever is right, whatever is pure, whatever is lovely, whatever is admirable—if anything is excellent or praiseworthy—think about such things.

We can only do this by spending a lot of time with our children and by making their intellectual, spiritual, and social development our top priority. Being a kid's mom and a kid's dad is work. It's not easy or convenient. And it's not always fun. But if it is true that nothing worthwhile comes easy, and that few things are more worthwhile than "training a child in the way he should go," then raising a child properly will be one of the most demanding jobs in the world. It's a good thing God has not left us on our own to do it.

I am continually amazed that the one who has become known as our "national mommy" has gained that stature because she discovered God and His objective moral standard through her own motherhood and family relationships. She now devotes her life to helping the whole country restore the primacy of family; the importance of marital fidelity; the holiness, grandeur, and indispensability of parenthood.

"I Am My Kid's Mom" is now a household phrase. It's on T-shirts and coffee mugs everywhere—I wouldn't be surprised if Dr. Laura even has it inscribed on her headstone! And why not? It's something worth being remembered for.

Truly, children are our greatest legacy, no matter how long we live! For nothing else we could ever do has the same potential for goodness and achievement that our children will have throughout their lives. The things they themselves will do and the influence they will exert within their own families and communities some day is greater than we can imagine.

Mothers are "not on the periphery of society," writes Meghan Cox Gurden, "we are at the center of it."[5] They always have been. The "hand that rocks the cradle" still rules the world.

Dr. Laura and the Christian Community

Oh, please! Grumbling about Dr. Laura is sort of like complaining about ice cream because it is not a good source of vitamin C. No, she's not a Christian, and yes, her answers are occasionally "blunt" and "arbitrary." She is, however, a refreshing light that shines brilliantly through some very nasty darkness. At a time when our culture is sinking in the mire, we need to encourage every voice that speaks unequivocally for traditional morality. To disparage her considerable influence for good is to show the very lack of grace you chide her for. Would you really want to leave the field to Howard Stern and his ilk?

Eleanor K. Gustafson's editorial response to a Christian's
negative review of Dr. Laura in World *magazine*

Irreconcilable Differences

I've always been intrigued by the wide range of opinions expressed by the Christian community about Dr. Laura and her program. As I looked through the archives at *World* magazine, an on-line Christian publication, I found two articles that were positive and two that were negative. The positive articles zeroed in on areas of agreement between Dr. Laura's beliefs and basic Christian values. The negative articles acknowledged those aspects *briefly*, and then focused on specific doctrinal differences that exist between Christianity and Judaism.

The congregation where I preach seems to be pretty typical of this kind of response. Many of our members are daily listeners of the show. There is widespread appreciation for the general morality and personal accountability she calls for. A few, however, are uncomfortable if I cite even one of her phone calls or monologues as a sermon illustration, even if the illustration fits exactly with Scripture. If I do,

I am invariably reminded after the service that she "doesn't accept Christ or understand grace."

No, she doesn't accept Jesus as the Messiah prophesied about in Old Testament Scripture. And, yes, she's a conservative Jew. Her views on what makes a person holy before God—her understanding of justification and sanctification—are therefore going to be different from ours. If one doesn't accept the New Testament as being authoritative in the same way one accepts the Old Testament, then naturally one's views on faith, works, grace, the kingdom of God, and many other doctrines will be different.

While doctrinal differences are very important, we need to keep the proper perspective on all of this as it relates to Dr. Laura's program. Hers is *not* a theological radio show. Her program may have an ever-increasing religious tone, but it's still not a religious program. It's not doctrinal instruction for believers, though a biblical passage here or there occasionally comes under scrutiny. She is a social activist who uses the Judeo-Christian Scriptures as the ethical platform from which she urges much-needed reforms.

The religious content of her program "comes into play" in two ways:

First, her broadcast is a daily invitation for an increasingly secular and godless society to take a serious look at God and His commandments as the solution to its problems.

Second, she supports, encourages, and invites all believers in God to take a stand with her as she carries on her "mission." She fights every day against evil of all kinds and, in particular, the evils that destroy families and children.

Does one have to be a Christian to do this? Does one have to understand the Bible perfectly before he or she can recommend its most fundamental precepts? Must one understand the Bible in precisely the same way other religions do before standing up to say, "Hey, we all need to take a look at this. This is good stuff!" Would we feel better if she *hadn't* written a *New York Times* best-seller on the Ten Commandments? Would we rather she anchor her approach to the "Egyptian Book of the Dead"?

A Cornered Market?

One of the articles I read in the September 20, 1997, issue of *World Magazine* was written by J. B. Cheaney and titled "Soul Food—But Can It Save?" It closed with this statement: "When it comes to spiritual matters, she [Dr. Laura] has nothing to tell me. God has said it all."

I've heard that from a few Christians I know. My publisher, who has received the occasional negative bit of criticism ("You're doing a positive Christian book on a Jewish person?"), has heard it too.

In answer to this, I would say that we need to remember that the power of God's Word lies not in the messenger but in the truth of the Word itself. Christians don't have the market cornered on scriptural, spiritual truths. God does! All truth is His truth whenever we hear it or wherever we find it. Whoever speaks it.

Read the following monologue carefully, and see if you don't think God can use a Jewish woman in the twentieth century for His purposes.

> *Dr. Laura:* J_____, welcome to the program.
> *Caller:* Hi.
> *Dr. Laura:* Hi!
> *Caller:* My problem is that I was raised in a family where religion was somewhat optional. And I know that sounds kind of funny. But we went to church on Christmas. You know, maybe once a year. And I guess I almost became . . . where I don't really believe it . . . because it wasn't really instilled in me as a child.
> *Dr. Laura:* Yeah, I understand that. I lived that. I didn't even get to church once a year.
> *Caller:* So my problem is, I have two small children, and I think that they should be raised with some sort of religion. And the problem that I'm having is that I feel really hypocritical bringing them to church when I myself don't actually believe.
> *Dr. Laura:* Oh, you're right. You would do just as much for them as your parents did for you.

Caller: Right.

Dr. Laura: You don't believe in God?

Caller: I believe in God.

Dr. Laura: Oh! Then what is it you don't believe in?

Caller: Well, I tend to believe that the stories in the Bible were stories to teach values and not meant to be taken literally. And you can't go to a Christian church and open your mouth and say something like that.

Dr. Laura: Well, the reality is, that you don't know if you're right.

Caller: Right. That's true.

Dr. Laura: You've *decided* that they're symbolic.

Caller: Right.

Dr. Laura: Well, they may or may not be. Because you've decided they are doesn't make them so.

Caller: Right.

Dr. Laura: And it could be that some of them are literal and some of them aren't and we don't know which ones. Could be that too. But when you make a statement that none of them are, that's a *faith* too.

Caller: Right. I understand that.

Dr. Laura: OK. So that means there's stuff to learn.

Caller: Well, there's always stuff to learn.

Dr. Laura: Right. So I think you ought to start going to church. There are a lot of reasons to be in church.

Caller: OK.

Dr. Laura: You want to go over what some of them are?

Caller: Sure.

Dr. Laura: OK. When you're in church, are you in the mall?

Caller: No.

Dr. Laura: Are you in front of the TV set?

Caller: No.

Dr. Laura: Are you getting your hair done?

Caller: No.

Dr. Laura: Are you doing any materialistic, frivolous,

superficial things?

Caller: No.

Dr. Laura: No. You're taking time out to tap into the spiritual.

Caller: Right.

Dr. Laura: You're taking time out to focus on something beyond your mundane life, of the choices you make, and you have the opportunity to make a connection to something . . . greater than how you live normally—which often elevates you. I mean, I could go on for days. I could give a five-hour lecture on this, but I think there are tremendous things to be gained from going to church or synagogue.

Caller: Well, I don't even know what church.

Dr. Laura: That's why you go and find out. It isn't torture. Especially if you go to a Christian church. They have very nice music.

Caller: OK.

Dr. Laura: I don't know all your levels of resistance, but I think they have more to do with your parents. Not everybody who goes to that church sits there and buys absolutely everything they're told. Everybody struggles with something.

Caller: OK.

Dr. Laura: Every Jew struggles with something in the Torah. Every Christian struggles and suffers with something in the New Testament. That's part of it. It's a struggle. Nobody's perfect. Nobody has perfect faith. Nobody makes perfect decisions and choices. We have the opportunity to constantly expand ourselves and get more and more holy so that we're way above the animals and not just living for gratification and exercise. And it's part of that attitude that you nurture when you embrace your religion. Go out and buy some books. There are Christian theologians. Sit and read. You'll see they argue with each other.

Caller: I don't even know which church to go to. I mean . . .

Dr. Laura: Go to the one closest to your home as a start.
Caller: OK.
Dr. Laura: Buy books. Start reading. When I got into Judaism, that's the first thing I did is I started reading because I didn't know anything. I had no clue. You go to services. You take a class. I took a course in Judaism. You find out.
Caller: OK.
Dr. Laura: And you'll find things that you love, and you'll find things that you grumble at. And some of the things you grumble at you will eventually love, and some of them you will be at friendly disagreement with. But so what?
Caller: OK.
Dr. Laura: It is a movement toward the holy.
Caller: OK.
Dr. Laura: Does that makes sense?
Caller: Yeah.
Dr. Laura: OK. You sound more relieved.
Caller: Yeah.
Dr. Laura: Good. OK. Don't get all worked up over this. This is something beautiful. Take it that way.
Caller: Thank you.

Just look at all of the important principles Dr. Laura taught this young woman, and everybody else who was listening, about pursuing faith.

> When children grow up without religious instruction, a meaningful faith is much harder to find and develop later in life. It also leaves people ill-equipped to help their own children in this regard.
> One's subjective and uninformed opinion that biblical stories aren't true does not make them so.
> We should study and investigate the Scriptures for ourselves before making up our minds about them.
> People need to go to church to "tap into" the spiritual side of life.

Just because we struggle with believing certain things
about our faith does not mean we shouldn't pursue
faith at all.

Everybody struggles.

We need to grow spiritually to elevate ourselves above
the animal and materialistic side of life.

God's laws will affect our lives in a positive way.

There will be much to love and appreciate as we grow
in spiritual matters.

Now let's be honest here. Hasn't God already said all of the above? Of course He has. Is it any less true because a Jewish woman said it? Of course not. But let me add one more question. Am I suggesting that we should just accept as biblical everything Dr. Laura "preaches, teaches, and nags"? Absolutely not. Dr. Laura is not infallible; she can and does make mistakes like the rest of us. She's on a spiritual journey and doesn't claim to know all truth. So, like the "noble-minded" Bereans of the first century, we should always "examine the Scriptures daily," to see whether the morality and precepts Dr. Laura espouses match with Scripture.

Common Ground Unfortunately, many in the Christ-believing community have done a disservice by "divorcing" the Old from the New Testament and by failing to appreciate the Jewish heritage of our faith. Maybe Dr. Laura will help provide some motivation for us to roll up our sleeves and correct this oversight. In fact, I'm starting to hear about Jewish and Christian groups getting together to explore all of their common religious ground. That can only help.

Perhaps we've forgotten (or just haven't thought about it) that Jesus lived His entire life fulfilling the Law of Moses. The record of the Christian church really doesn't begin until the book of Acts. Acts 2 is the first instance where people first came into the "new covenant relationship" with God through their faith in Jesus the Christ.

So what is a *Christ*-ian exactly? Isn't it someone who has been redeemed, forgiven, justified by faith in Christ's atoning work on the cross? Someone who has been declared righteous by God on the grounds of this grace? Someone who is empowered by His Spirit to follow Him? His teaching? His example? Jesus' teaching illuminated the moral integrity of Mosaic Law. His life was lived in perfect harmony with God's commandments. And so the less we know about God's dealings with His chosen people, the less we will know about our own faith and Lord.

Jim McGuiggan, author and scholar from Northern Ireland, once wrote the following to me:

> I'm glad you're interested in the Old Testament because, among many other reasons, it's Act 1 in a two-act drama (the drama continues even now, as you're well aware). To go to a play as Act 2 is beginning is a severe disadvantage. The characters are already developed, the movement of the plot is already underway—why Elsie struck Wilma, how it is that Joe stands as heir rather than Harry, why the council is so opposed to the building project of William, and how it is that Nora is not really the daughter of Clara and John—is all to be guessed at. It's more than missing information; it's a loss of tone, complexion, spirit of the whole movement of the drama.

I've read so many times in Luke 2 about how Jesus went to the temple with His family when He was twelve years old. How He asked and answered questions of the teachers there and made such an impression on everybody. But I never really "saw" what was going on until I attended my first bar mitzvah. Now I have an entirely different perspective and a whole new appreciation of what was taking place. Jesus was taking His place in the community of Israel's men, gaining the right to read publicly from the books of the Torah, and engaging the teachers, not as a boy, but as a man.

Of course, Jesus didn't just follow the Law; as its author and fulfillment, He superseded it. That's why the New Testament emphasizes the "law of Christ," not the "law of Moses." Christians believe Jesus was the Messiah prophesied about in the Old Testament. We believe the covenant that God made with Israel at Sinai was replaced. No longer does God relate specifically with one nation with whom He had made a covenant at Sinai; now He calls His own all who have a relationship with Him based on their faith that Jesus is the Son of God.

Having said all that, I want to emphasize that just because Christians believe the old covenant has been superseded by the new, that doesn't mean that much in the Old Testament is not still relevant for us. In Romans 15:4, Paul said:

> For everything that was written in the past was written to teach us, so that through endurance and the encouragement of the Scriptures we might have hope.

Paul was talking about the Old Testament Scriptures here. He said that the patience and encouragement they would impart as we *learned* them would give us hope. What hope? The same hope the rest of the New Testament speaks of. Life with God through faith in Christ.

The same fundamental moral principles, the ethical underpinnings, embodied in the Ten Commandments and the moral laws from the Pentateuch are consistent with those in the New Testament. That is why the Old Testament still gives us hope today. That is why the Ten Commandments and other Old Testament Scriptures are referenced frequently throughout the New Testament. We still need many of its precepts. Here are just a few examples:

> Let no debt remain outstanding, except the continuing debt to love one another, for he who loves his fellowman has fulfilled the law. The commandments, "Do not commit adultery," "Do not murder," "Do not steal," "Do not covet," and whatever other commandment there may be, are summed up in this one rule: "Love your neighbor as yourself." Love does no harm to its neighbor. Therefore

love is the fulfillment of the law. (Romans 13:8–10; see also Exodus 20:14-17; Leviticus 19:18)

Children, obey your parents in the Lord, for this is right. "Honor your father and mother"—which is the first commandment with a promise—"that it may go well with you and that you may enjoy long life on the earth." (Ephesians 6:1–2; see also Exodus 20:12; Deuteronomy 4:40)

For the Scripture says, "Do not muzzle the ox while it is treading out the grain," and "The worker deserves his wages." (1 Timothy 5:18; see also Deuteronomy 25:4; 24:15)

I haven't been calling the Scriptures the Judeo-Christian Bible throughout this book for nothing! Whatever Old and New Testament truths Dr. Laura teaches—and she teaches much from both—we should be grateful that God's voice is being heard.

"A Close Brush with Christianity"

Rather than dwell on the negative criticism she occasionally receives from the Christian community, Dr. Laura prefers to accentuate the positive relationships she has with Christians. She received a lot of encouragement just a little over two years ago and was quite overwhelmed by it.

I had a close brush with Christianity over the weekend, and I want to say thank you publicly to someone, because I was so incredibly touched. As you know, there's a sharkfest of gossip going around, impugning my entire character by saying that I was rude and offensive to an audience during a public speaking engagement. What's kind of funny about this is twenty-five years of working in the public, one incident happens, or seems to happen, or is purported to happen, and twenty-five years of your history become meaningless. And I'll tell you why. It's everything from competitiveness to envy to smarminess to a desire for ratings.

So it's been a feeding frenzy for radio talk shows, newspapers, magazines, news, and TV shows who just live for scum. Somebody told me just the other day not to worry about this, because if Mother Teresa had tripped over a dog, it would be published that she kicked an animal. That's more exciting than "she tripped over a dog." I've got news for you. God's got a lot of elves out there, but the Devil has too . . . Any which way, I wanted to give a public thank-you.

I never call in my office answering machine on the weekends. Never. But something compelled me to do it this weekend, and it was loaded to the rafters, which also never happens because we don't give out the number on the air. I could not figure out how the phone system could be so totally locked up. You couldn't have added another call. So I'm listening to one right after the other: "I'm a Christian, and I just want you to know that this nonsense is . . . and I'm praying for you." "I'm a Christian . . ."

What? Where is this coming from? Turns out there is a gentleman on a Christian broadcasting station in Southern California. His name is Warren Duffy. It's called "Duffy and Company." He went on the air and said he knew of my work and he has heard of my character, and whatever the gossip was, it had to be a distortion and untrue. "She must be in great pain and needs our support. Here's her phone number. Call her. It's the Christian thing to do."

So I'm deluged with these calls. I'm listening to them, you know. Fifteen, twenty minutes into listening to these messages, and I'm sobbing all over the place because of the kind things that people were saying. So I just wanted to say thank you publicly.

This monologue did more than demonstrate Dr. Laura's appreciation for the Christian community. It also pointed to something with which we Christians are also familiar: persecution.

Persecution

When one attains the stature and influence Dr. Laura has as a social and moral activist, critics just can't wait for the slightest slipup to occur—real or imagined. In fact, anyone who's listened to the show for long has probably noticed the invective increasing with her growing popularity.

It is sad, but not surprising, that a person can be a vanguard for any kind of moral perversion but not receive the criticism or scrutiny that a decent, moral person does. Take a stand for objective morality and simple goodness, and it's open season. Since Dr. Laura's approach has become ethically based and rooted to the Judeo-Christian Bible, she has begun to experience the same fierce opposition that many a religious teacher has before her.

This is not just something that's going to get worse before it gets better; this is another reason all who believe in God need to start banding together on our common ground so that we can more effectively influence society.

Christians understand the attacks Dr. Laura has regularly encountered since she has been in the limelight. People who stand for traditional morality and goodness have been intentionally and dishonestly demonized for years. A strategy that, it would appear, has met with more than a little success.

Taking Clergy to Task

If Dr. Laura is nondenominational in her positive promotion of God and God's law to society, she is equally nondenominational in her bone-picking with religious leaders.

One of the reasons America is in spiritual and moral decline is because its spiritual leaders have abdicated their responsibility. Like ancient Israel, America grew to be great and prosperous because of the goodness the faith of its hardworking people inspired. And like ancient Israel, the further America gets away from God, the more problems it causes for itself.

One of the first groups God sent prophets to preach repentance to was religious leaders. The shepherds of Israel had refused to tend the flock God had entrusted to them. There is no question that whenever and wherever spiritual leaders fail in their responsibilities, the ones they lead become weak, incapable of living the kind of lives God has called them to. And if we are too weak to live correctly ourselves, how can we possibly influence others for good?

One of the most scathing rebukes of these leaders came from the prophet Ezekiel:

> The word of the Lord came to me: "Son of man, prophesy against the shepherds of Israel; prophesy and say to them: 'This is what the Sovereign Lord says: Woe to the shepherds of Israel who only take care of themselves! Should not shepherds take care of the flock? You eat the curds, clothe yourselves with the wool and slaughter the choice animals, but you do not take care of the flock. You have not strengthened the weak or healed the sick or bound up the injured. You have not brought back the strays or searched for the lost. You have ruled them harshly and brutally. So they were scattered because there was no shepherd, and when they were scattered they became food for all the wild animals. My sheep wandered over all the mountains and on every high hill. They were scattered over the whole earth, and no one searched or looked for them.
>
> ". . . This is what the Sovereign Lord says: I am against the shepherds and will hold them accountable for my flock." (Ezekiel 34:1–6, 10)

What happened to the spiritual leaders? They ceased to really care about the people. They lost their conviction and compassion. They who had become spiritually superficial and worldly were leading others down the same path. They became self-serving—put their own wants and needs ahead of the flock. The flock was weak, sickly, injured, and lost, and they were left to perish. What authority the leaders did exercise was not for benevolent purposes; it was a harsh, brutal, and egotistical expression of self-glory. God was going to call each of them to account.

What do you say about spiritual leaders that are neither spiritual nor leaders?

Here's what Dr. Laura would say. Dr. Laura's running commentary is in italics.

One of the things that I am pleased that I have been able to do on this program is to beg, plead, nag, cajole, nag, remind, irritate, and nag clergy. I don't care what denomination. I don't care what religion. I'm nagging all of you. I'm nondenominational in my clerical nagging. To uphold the standards and not be a camp counselor. See, I think too many priests, rabbis, and ministers are camp counselors instead of leaders. We have something from a priest here . . . we get a lot of these every day. I just pick out what I think are the cream of the cream.

He says, "Some time ago, I began to realize that I was not always serving people as well as I could. You had suggested in the past that sometimes clergy might not be doing their jobs because they are concerned with keeping the pews filled. That may sometimes be so. I suggest a few other factors may be even more important. It is easier to keep silent under the guise of compassion than to speak the truth that people need to hear, so that they might free themselves with God's help from the self-imposed burdens"—*self-imposed burdens*—"that bring so much sadness and misery to their own lives and to the lives of other people. This umbrella of false compassion can also protect you from having to look too closely at your own faults. Because if you readily excuse and justify the actions of others when they come to you for help, it makes it easier to excuse your own faults."

That is very true, and that is very telling. That's why, in this day and age, we have a lot of people walking around, since the sixties, going, "You shouldn't judge anybody." You know what they're doing? They're laying the groundwork so they won't be judged. They're willing to sacrifice anything else going on so their tushies are covered. I continue on.

"I think too often today when people come to a priest seeking advice, he may not want to 'add to their burden' or 'make them feel guilty,' or perhaps it is more important for him to be seen as a kind, caring sort of guy. So he leaves individuals without a challenge, without applying God's law, and without any real tools to improve their lives. They both feel better when they're done meeting, but neither one is any better in the end.

"To offer a cup of coffee might be a greater kindness. But to speak the truth because you care, even if it's hard to take and even if it pricks your own conscience, gives people a basis for action and a hope for the possibility of real change. God can do a lot of work with both of us, under those circumstances. I also think it pushes the priest, like it or not, to a deeper and more authentic compassion for those people and challenges him to live better the same truth that he speaks to others. It's hard for us, too, but there is no other way. And no better way. The greatest idolatry today is egotism."

Oh, this man and I are of one mind. Whew. "It's our job as priests and clergy of all faiths to show people there is only one God—and it ain't us." *That's very good.* "If we walk along His path, our lives may not always be happy, but they can be very, very good. This kind of life is really worth living."

This is a man and a priest who has really examined himself. I would trust going to him for religious advice. Doesn't matter we're not of the same religion. We've got the same . . . concept. And if you're getting less than that, if you're getting clergy who are voting on what is now moral because they don't want to hurt somebody's feelings, then you know it has moved away from religion and become a camp. And they're the counselor, and they want all the little counselees to be happy. Not healthy, not holy—just happy.

Struggling with "Bits and Pieces" of Scripture

An atheist called in one day looking for spiritual direction. Now that he had children, he felt the need to provide opportunities for their spiritual growth, opportunities he did not have as a child. Dr. Laura's constant nagging about how important religion is to a family was getting to him. But as he and the kids began to attend the church his wife grew up in, he found himself uncomfortable with some of the things taught there. He didn't really agree with all that he heard and was searching for a handle on what really was true or not.

It can be hard to become informed because, as Dr. Laura told him, "It just seems sometimes that people are gathered into the church, and then they have somebody who pulls things out of context for the theme of the day."

As a minister, I thought, "Ouch!" But there is a lot of truth in what she said. She continued:

> Part of the reason [in going to church] is to study the Scriptures and try to make sense of them in terms of what is expected of us in our daily behavior. These things are written several thousand years ago in an entirely different world. But they hold truths which are universal. So, yes. You need to take bits and pieces and try to make sense out of them to see what God expects of you and how you're supposed to behave, what your obligations are to your family, to your community, and to God. How else would you do that if you don't study and discuss them? I think you want it to be too simple, like a how-to book. You want it to be real clear and not have any disputes. But it's impossible. We struggle with these things. God is not e-mailing us today. We have to struggle with the Word and try to make sense of it, understanding that these things were written in a different context two thousand

years ago. And for me, longer than that because I'm Jewish. So it requires constant education.

Yes, it does. Whenever I'm seeking the true biblical perspective on any issue, I remind myself once again that a little knowledge is a dangerous thing. If one is going to study the Bible, one should undertake to do it properly and to the best of one's ability. It will take self-discipline, persistence, and systematic endeavor to do it well. But the lack of organization and commitment, and the failure to apply good old-fashioned elbow grease to the Scriptures, has made the Bible the most quoted and least understood book in history.

Dr. Laura is correct; we need to study the Scriptures, struggle to find meaning in the bits and pieces so we can know what God expects of us. Gordon Fee and Douglas Stuart, in their excellent book *How to Read the Bible for All Its Worth*, say it this way:

> Because the Bible is God's Word, it has eternal relevance; it speaks to all mankind, in every age and in every culture. . . . But because God chose to speak His Word through human words in history, every book in the Bible also has historical particularity; each document is conditioned by the language, time, and culture in which it was originally written. . . . Interpretation of the Bible is demanded by the "tension" that exists between its eternal relevance and its historical particularity.[1]

| Final Thoughts | Through the prophet Isaiah, God tells us about the effectiveness of His words: |

As the rain and the snow
   come down from heaven,
and do not return to it
   without watering the earth
and making it bud and flourish,
   so that it yields seed for the sower and

bread for the eater, so is my word that goes out from my mouth:
It will not return to me empty,
but will accomplish what I desire
and achieve the purpose for which I sent it. (Isaiah 55:10–11)

Isaiah's reminder of the strength, wisdom, and effectiveness of God's Word helps me keep the benefits of Dr. Laura's program in perspective. The biblical truths she proclaims over the airwaves and in her magazine and books will indeed accomplish what God desires and achieve the purpose for which He sent it. This book has hopefully made that a little more obvious as we've examined her exhortations:

- To believe in God.
- To embrace God's commandments as an absolute, workable, ethical standard upon which our society can "hang its hat."
- Appealing to character, courage, and conscience as a more pragmatic solution to life's problems than moral relativism and pop psychology.
- See a lot of the current social trends/ideas for what they are— destructive to relationships as God intended for them to be and devastating to children.
- For all religious people to stand together where they share truth in common so that we can make the difference in our society that the Apostle Paul talks about in Philippians 2:12–16:

Therefore, my dear friends, as you have always obeyed— not only in my presence, but now much more in my absence—continue to work out your salvation with fear and trembling, for it is God who works in you to will and to act according to his good purpose. Do everything without complaining or arguing, so that you may be- come blameless and pure, children of God without fault in a crooked and depraved generation, in which you shine like stars in the universe as you hold out the word of life.

So as I consider all that this "Mother in America" has done and is doing for millions of people all over the world, I will continue to be thankful to God for her conversion from atheism to Judaism.

Would she, could she have accomplished all that she has in the absence of faith? Without the God of Scripture in whom she now believes? No. I don't believe that, and I'm sure she doesn't either. She is diligently planting and watering, but it is God who is giving the increase.

That doesn't mean I won't continue to pray that one day she'll perceive that Jesus is the prophesied Messiah. Anyone who stands before God in judgment not believing in Jesus will have to stand alone—without Him as their advocate. I'm sure we'll chat about that from time to time as we have opportunity. Given the intellectual honesty she's demonstrated in changing her mind on issues of great import in the past, I don't think it would be that big of a leap for her. The Apostle Paul said that the law was a "schoolmaster . . . unto Christ" (Galatians 3:24, KJV). Since it still is, perhaps her journey as a relatively new convert has only just begun in more ways than she can now possibly imagine.

Some Funny Stuff

Poetry is a very enjoyable hobby of mine. Has been since high school. A poet's inspiration is where you find it, and I find a lot of it on Dr. Laura's program. A lot of calls and some of her monologues will sometimes tickle my funny bone while others just get my goat. Sitting at home in front of the fire on a number of evenings has resulted in some of the following. Others came to me so quickly I just tapped them out and faxed them to her, and she would read them the same day she made the comments that inspired them. It's been fun "teaming up" with her on the occasional issue in this way.

Nearly all of the following pieces were either read by Dr. Laura on the air or printed in her magazine, *The Dr. Laura Perspective*. I've been amazed at the number of calls from all over the country that our church office—and sometimes Dr. Laura's office from what I've heard—has received requesting copies of these. Now they have been made available in this book and I appreciate Chariot Victor allowing me to include them. The poetry in this section is various poems or parodies of well-known poems that were all inspired by something Dr. Laura mentioned on the air. I hope you enjoy reading them as much as I enjoyed writing them.

About Those Knocked-Up Brides . . .

Dear Dr. Laura,

I've often been amazed at the petty self-centeredness that manifests itself by many of the brides that call you and ask your advice on something. But this takes the cake. A pregger-bride actually throws a tantrum because her wedding dress doesn't fit due to her ever-expanding tummy and was blaming the dressmaker for it?!? And now some dressmakers have actually instituted a policy that insists pregnant brides sign waivers . . . sheesh! Only in America.

The Bride in the Tar Barrel Dress

I heard a bride, on a summer day,
Brisk and busy, and ripe for a quarrel;
Buzzing and bouncing right off of the wall,
In a gown the size of an old tar-barrel.

Do you ask what her buzzing was all about?
Was she being shrewd and analytical?
Why, 'twas sport to hear her scold and shout,
Oh she was wondrous rude and critical.

First and foremost she buzzed of size—overwrought,
And threatened the helpful bridal fitter;
Deceiving herself with silly lies—she thought,
"If she makes me look fat . . . I'll get her."

Because I hopped in the sack too soon,
Got knocked up—there'll be no doubt of it.
But I'm in love after all and he made me swoon,
I must appear pure—(though he cheated me out of it).

Then plaintive and piteous her humming grew,
And we thought her complaining of indigestion;
But we listened again and at length we knew,
She'd gained thirty pounds—no question.

"But the world," she declared, would watch in wonder,
And gaze at her while walking down the aisle.
No one would think she'd made a blunder.
(All stigma and shame has been gone for awhile).

Next, tones of fury and wrath were heard,
And the fitter jumped back in wonder;
For the snaps all popped and the seams all ripped,
With the violence and volume of thunder.

"'Tis a crime the way *YOU'VE* made me look!"
"'Tis a deed," she said, "most foul and ugly."
"How dare you ruin *MY* wedding day,
By making my gown fit so snugly!"

But the bridal gown maker found finally—success,
And presented the bill to the bride.
At which point the girl noted one whole, extra dress,
As her eyes grew first narrow—then wide.

"What's this?" she screamed, "there's only *ONE* dress."
"But you are clearly charging for two!"
"And that waiver I'm signing under duress . . .
And . . . I just can't believe the amount due!"

The dressmaker just smiled with a smile so uncanny,
And said, "Dear you'll have to make do.
'Cause it's not just a matter of covering your pregnant fanny. . .
. . . I have to cover mine too!"

(apologies to William Cullen Bryant, *The Bee in the Tar Barrel*, 1831)

Topless Equality with Men

Dear Dr. Laura,

Was pruning my hard drive this morning, when I came across this verse I penned earlier this year when I heard of that young, teenage, Eugene, Oregon, girl that was asserting her equality with men by going "topless" as men sometimes do—then being thoroughly bent out of shape because she was arrested for indecent exposure! Seems her logic went something like this. If her coworking men

on the road crew don't have to wear shirts, and women
are equal with men, then women shouldn't have to wear
shirts either. Makes sense to me!

Of Equal Rights and Mammaries

"God's country" it is called by some
In Oregon (Eugene),
Because of its great beauty there
Everything is lovely green.

But what IS this with girls up there?
Spouting feminist equalese,
Asserting "equal rights" with men
By flashing mammaries?!?

"It must be all the rain," he mused
As the article he read,
All that dampness, mold, and fungus
Must take root inside the head.

As a rule, men's pectorals
Aren't really all that great,
You have to be a Schwarzennegger
To really titillate.

But, let's face it—most us men
When we're out on the beach
Displaying chests all pale and hairy,
To every woman within reach

Don't really seem to overwhelm,
Much less thrill, enthrall.
See? The women are all just yawning.
No one's turned on at all.

But when it comes to women's chests,
Be they large or small or medium,
Just one glimpse of a woman's chest,
Is enough to break the tedium.

That's BECAUSE (now get a clue)
As a rule—they're fruit forbidden.
And for that reason, it's really best,
That in public they stay HIDDEN!

NOW Goes on the Warpath

Dear Dr. Laura,

Given the decline in modern education, many may not understand the following parody of Longfellow's *Hiawatha's Departure* from the *Song of Hiawatha*. But after hearing and reading all weekend how NOW went on the warpath against the Promise Keepers at their Washington rally, I suppose the following verse was inevitable . . .

"I Am Awful's" Departure

(From the Song of Iamawful)

On the streets of Gonna' Getcha',
At the Promise Keeper rally,
Down the street from Capi-tol-lee,
In the pleasant summer morning.
Iamawful stood and waited.
All the air was full of freshness,
All the earth was bright and joyous,
And before them through the sunshine,
Eastward toward the neighboring parcel,
Passed in teeming throngs the menfolk,
Passed the males, the Promise-Keepers,
Praying, singing in the sunshine.
The insipid Iamawful,
With her hands aloft extended,
Held aloft the signs insipid,
Plastered with the dumb invective,

'Til the messages on placards,
Grated on the whining warriors,
Stranded on the concrete margin,
Till a camera from the station,
With the promise of exposure,
Landed on the concrete margin.
Then the maddened Iamawful
Cried aloud and spake in this wise:
"Oh we hate these strangers, these guys,
All our group in hate awaits them,
In our wigwams we berate them,
All our women stand against them,
With our heart's right hand we'll slap them."
For their promises are scary,
For of virtue we are wary,
And our hatchets we would bury,
In those backs that are so hairy.
From the margin shrill and ceaseless,
Rose a cry of curse and peaceless,
Iamawful's stern agenda,
Came unto a fruitless enda.
Some dozen squaws of NOW then,
Came to Washington to wow them,
Came to Washington to floor them,
With a cry, "We're off to war then,
And proceeded then to bore them.
But it seemed to us who watched it,
That the NOW tribe really botched it,
For they showed just what they're made of,
As they spoke of what they're 'fraid of,
The nation stood and viewed them,
As they fussed and fumed and stewed in,
All throughout their teeny gathering,
While their teeny efforts lathering.
While engaged in verbal violence,
'Til they sank into the silence,

While we said, "Farewell forever!"
Why, we hope to see you never,
Bade farewell to NOW forever . . .

(apologies to Henry Wadsworth Longfellow)

But It Feels So Natural!

Well Dr. Laura,
Your show did it again . . . jump-started the poet-laureate within and inspired me to more bulletin material (but it's not Sunday yet so you get the material before the congregation does!). Your conversation yesterday with the guy who, after one WHOLE MONTH, was feeling so "naturally amorous," that he wondered when it would be "right" for sex to enter the picture . . . I must admit your (spontaneous) depiction of one "squatting" being a natural, (animal?) thing to do—made the point rather graphically and gave rise to the following . . .

If it *feels* good *just do it*—it feels oh so natural,
A chief aim in life—catering to the infatual.
And so to defer—to those instincts of mine,
Requires me only—to draw my own line.

In drawing my line—putting ME at the center,
Simplifies things—no virtue need enter.
It's only the need of the moment that's counting,
The pressure to biblically know you is mounting.

The obvious pun of course—is intended,
Since we're "kindred spirits"—there's no one offended!
We'll just acquiesce to—what "feels just so right,"
Smoke a joint—pop a pill—"Hey it's late . . . spend the night!"

If it feels good just do it—it feels oh so natural,
A chief aim in life—catering to the infatual.

For example when burping—you do it so loudly,
That all your good buddies—will point to you proudly.

There's a problem of course—with this lower view,
Ya' look and act like . . . well, ever been to the zoo?
There you will find—just all sorts of critters,
Doin' what's natural—though it gives us the jitters.

For example the exhibit—what's it called, Archipelago?
That our whole family visited—just a short while ago?
There—to my young son's and teenage daughter's dismay,
Every tortoise in view—was bumpin' away.

"What's goin' on?"—my young innocent asked,
As wide-eyed he viewed—turtles bent to their task.
Why are they stacked with their tongues hangin' out—what's
    the reason?
"Simple, my son," I replied—"They're in season."

"Oooohhh gross!" said my daughter—was all she could say,
Every turtle in view was mating that day.
But as I explained—"It's perfectly natural."
"What you're seeing right now—in nature is actual!"

"Let's go see the monkeys," said my young man.
"This is disgusting!—I've seen all that I can!"
Then he bounded with joy to the cage marked "Primate"
With rapt fascination . . . 'til he saw what they ate!

This simian squatted and left a huge pile,
Which he scooped with his finger and sucked, with a smile.
"GROSS!" squealed the daughter—"ICK!" yelled the son.
While I smiled at my wife—who said, "Isn't THIS fun?"

But what disgusts us is backwards!—This makes us feel sick???
This behavior in animals—that makes us go ICK!
But it is oh so natural—so what is the fuss?
Those disgusting gross animals—acting ***better*** than us!

For they do what they do—with no other choice.
'Tis instinct that drives them—they haven't a voice,
Of reason or conscience—Like all of us do!
But we look *worse* than monkeys—when we act like them too!

The point being of course—should be easy to see.
I COULD act like an animal—and focus on me.
But to go AGAINST nature—with behavior sublime
Uplifts and ennobles—and helps me to climb.

To a much higher plane of existence—guess what?
That's what I was made for—no if and or but.
To fend off the "feelings"—to fight the subjective,
And embrace what is virtue—what is good—the objective.

To impart the true meaning—the quintessentially spiritual
To what'd otherwise be—mere animal ritual
If it FEELS good just do it! is the worst slogan EVER
Let's try . . . "If it IS good just do it!"—'tis more noble
   (and clever!)

Characterlessitis . . .

Dear Dr. Laura,

I was amused at your comments about the communicability of the new "disease" you referred to yesterday (the cocaine councilman), as you mentioned the need to close the windows lest your family become infected. You then stated it was a question of being characterless . . . which gave rise to the following thoughts and rhyme . .

DICTIONARY REF. A FEW YEARS FROM NOW???

Characterlessitis—(kare'-ekter-le-site'-us) *noun* 1. A disease caused by a missing or defective gene which results in a severe deficiency of character, courage, and conscience. 2. Criminal activity aggravated by victimization syndrome [see societal disorders]

I used to think the only thing—that I might catch by breathin'
Would be perhaps the common cold—by some infected
  heathen.
But now I find that something worse, than burs- or arthir- itis
Now permeates society—it's CHARACTERLESSITIS!

"Of course!" I thought, "that would explain—the recent
  epidemic
The rash of immorality—that's become so darned endemic.
And despite the work of Dr. Laura's virtuous polemic
Characterlessitis has become it seems—systemic.

The symptoms of this malady—are nought at which to sneeze
Considering politicians are ex-pert on this disease.
Why, they can tell you instantly—with complete conviction
Cocaine habits can't be helped—we're victims of addiction.

Please note the word's root origins—"A piece of chalk now,
  please."
The prefix *"dis"* as in *dis*miss—morality for sleaze.
And now, you'll note, the suffix here—"E—A—S—E" *ease*
As in "effortlessly" chalking all of—this up to disease.

The really "sickening" thing in this—impromptu diagnostic
Shows how our leading citizens—are morally agnostic
Yes shining, great examples of—civic pride and service.
They're not "bad," they just got "sick"—now don't that make
  you nervous?

So batten down them hatches, boys—Shut those windows,
  bolt those doors
Can't run the risk of breathin' in—incriminalizing spores.
Until they pioneer vaccine—to protect us from this germ.
Which reduces us so helplessly—to the morals of a worm.

So beware this new disease—called characterlessitis!
So contagious that I'll bet—it's already now inside us

Like a cancer nibbling 'way—at virtue and at will.
Why . . . I feel some symptoms coming on—I'm off to rob a
    till!

Dear Dr. Laura,
I couldn't help but think of Ernest Lawrence Thayer's
immortal classic, "Casey at the Bat," after listening to you
"strike out" at the top of the hour yesterday. What an
unbelievable caller. While you finally got through to the
first couple of callers (by pulling hen's teeth), you didn't
even make a dent in that third guy. Well, no one bats a
thousand I suppose . . . it *did* seem like there was a full
moon out yesterday.

Dr. Laura at the Mike

The outlook wasn't brilliant for the callers nine that day,
'Twas like pulling teeth for Carolyn—to see what they had
    to say.
And then when caller one spaced out—and caller two did
    much the same;
A sickly silence fell upon the listeners of the game.

A straggling few reached o'er to turn—their AM radios off.
    The rest,
Clung to that hope which springs eternal in the human breast.
They thought if Dr. Laura could—cut through all that pop-
    psych
We'd put up money even now—with Dr. Laura at the mike!

But Dense preceded Airhead, as did also Slimeball Sam,
The former, simply clueless—the latter didn't give a darn!
So upon the stricken listeners, grim melancholy spread;
It seemed that hardly anyone—would key to what she said.

But Dense—she finally listened—to the wonderment of all!

And Sam, though much despised by now—tore the cover off
   his gall.
And when the fog had lifted—the listeners knew what had
   occurred;
There was Dense all straightened out—And Slimeball Sam
   deferred!

Then from the untold thousands, there arose a lusty yell,
'Twas heard clear up to Heaven and—down to the gates of
   Heck!
The listener's all yelled "sic 'em"—the caller next in line
   thought, "YIKE!"
For Laura, Doctor Laura—was leaning toward the mike.
There was ease in Dr. Laura's voice—she said, "Welcome to
   the show."
There was confidence in her voice just when—she said, "I
   know, I know!"
And when she stated firmly—"My opinion you may not
   like."
No stranger on the airwaves could doubt—'Twas Dr. Laura
   at the mike!

Ten thousand ears were on her as she cut right to the chase,
Five thousand tongues applauded when she got right in his
   face!
Then while the writhing caller squirmed, tried to wiggle off
   the "hook,"
Dr. Laura bored right in—"You're going to be in my next
   book!"

The flimsy-covered rationales—came hurtling through the air,
And Dr. Laura sat a-listening—righteous indignation there.
Right at the sturdy counselor—the excuses unheeded sped,
"YOU HAVE GOT TO BE KIDDING ME!"—"Strike
   one," the screener said.

From the airwaves, thick with people, there went up a muffled
   roar,

Like the beating of the storm-waves on a stern and distant
    shore.
"Disconnect him! Disconnect the bum!"—The show's producer
    made demand.
It's likely they'd disconnected him—had not Laura raised
    her hand.

With a sigh of Jewish—patience, Dr. Laura's visage shone,
She said with calm, "Now take deep breaths!"—After the
    break—we will go on.
Then afterwards, she laid it out—"This is what you HAVE
    TO DO!"
The caller still ignored her—and Larry mouthed, "Strike two."

"Fraud!" cried the maddened listeners, and the echo answered,
    "Fraud!"
But one scornful chide from Laura—and the audience was
    awed.
They heard her voice grow stern and cold, they listened to
    her logic,
They knew this Slime just had to crack—no matter how
    mysogic.

The lilt is gone from Laura's voice, her hair begins to spike;
She raps with cruel violence, her knuckles on the mike.
And now she bangs the console! And now she shouts,
    "HELLOOO!?!"
And now the airwaves shatter from the force of Laura's blow
    . . . (click)

Oh, somewhere in this favored land, the sun is shining bright,
The band is playing somewhere, and somewhere hearts are light.
And somewhere men are upright, and somewhere families
    shout,
But there is no joy at KFI—Doctor Laura has struck out!

(apologies to Ernest Lawrence Thayer)

193

Character Pill

Dear Dr. Laura,

Couldn't resist! You said at the top of the show, something about "Wouldn't it be nice if we could just take a character pill?" I thought, "Hah! Who would wanna take it and quit misbehaving?" On second thought . . .

You find the chemist . . . I'll handle the promotional.

Character Pill

Character has self-imploded
Anachronistically outmoded
That's why there ain't no character pill
'Cause we don't need it. We ain't ill

And even if someone could make it
Good luck getting some to take it
Not e'en placebos could cut it here
'Cause goody-two-shoes looks we fear

Since right's now wrong and wrong's now right
We won't take it without a fight
We won't take one no time soon
Not even in a jelly-spoon

But wait, just wait! I had a thought
Of how to make this character sought
To make character ameliorating
And virtue pills non-expectorating

We would take them without a fuss,
If you would advertise them thus . . .

"Step right up, folks, this here dose
Will make you so much less morose
Don't need to change no state of mind
Just swallow this and you'll feel fine"

"Step right up, folks, this here pill
Will make you gorgeous, yes, it will

Will melt off pounds, will make you thin
In Hollywood it's really 'in'"

"Are you bald, do you lack hair
Need more follicles here and there?"
Just swallow one of these per day
The babes—they will not stay away

"Are you too hairy in many places?"
"Are you ashamed to smile with braces?"
"Do you have one of those ugly faces?"
This pill will cover all those bases!

And one more thing I must disclose
If you really want that perfect nose
Just take this pill and take it now
Then we will ogle you, and HOW!

So someone please invent this pill
We've found the way, we've found the will
You'll take it without realizing
You got sucked in through ADVERTISING!

I faxed the following list to Dr. Laura after she specifically made a request for clergymen to send her their "Ten Stupid Things Ministers Do to Mess Up Their Congregations" for a special edition of her newsletter. Alas, truth is not only stranger than fiction, it is funnier. All of the following are true except number 3 (which I've only thought about doing). I have to personally confess to numbers 4, 6, and 10 (7 was a near-miss!). The rest have all happened to friends and colleagues of mine.

Ten Stupid Things Ministers Do To Mess Up Their Congregations

The Lighter Side

Stupid Timing

1. Wait for a cold morning in the dead of winter when the heater's broken to preach a sermon on hell (when they actually wish they could be there)
   OR WORSE

2. Show up an hour late on daylight saving time weekend when your sermon board in front of the church has been announcing the sermon all week, "Be Prepared"

Stupid Technology

3. Cranking the water heater thermostat to max, then using your cell phone and notebook computer to get your work done while you take a Jacuzzi in the baptistery

Stupid Visits to the Hospital

4. Go to visit a parishioner in ICU who's just been in a horrible accident, is in traction and bandages up to his eyeballs, and start the conversation by asking, "So, how have you been?"

Stupid Scripture Reading

5. Put the wrong emphasis AND misplace the comma when reading Ephesians 4:28, "Let him who stole steal, no longer working with his hands what is good . . . "

Stupid Repetition

6. While preaching a sermon on evolution and creation, use the phrase "testable hypothesis" ONCE too many times . . . (use your imagination here) which, aside from leaving the congregation wondering what the heck kinda' hypothesis is THAT ???—gives the minister a grand view of 100 pairs of tonsils simultaneously!

Stupid Transportation

7. Offering a ride home to an "L.O.L." (little old lady) after the women's midweek Bible study, only to escort her to the parking lot and remember that you brought the motorcycle to work that day.

Stupid Missionary Faux Pas

8. When preaching in a Third World country, you avert your gaze to the other side of the assembly because a beautiful young girl has dropped her top to nurse her baby, then you concentrate on the center aisle because another woman is doing the same on the other side—only to see a woman in the back and center nursing TWINS! (actually this goes in the list of Ten stupid things congregations do to mess up ministers).

Stupid Double Standards

9. Fall asleep during the announcements just before you are introduced when your sermon that morning is all about paying better and more respectful attention in the worship services
   OR WORSE
10. Christian ministers who will preach on Sunday about where the Jews have "missed it," and on weekdays, fax Jewish radio talk show hosts.

Endnotes

Chapter 1: The Appeal of Dr. Laura

1. Anita Manning, "Dr. Laura Dispenses Morality Over the Radio," *USA Today*, September 25, 1997.

2. Arsenio Orteza, "Talk Radio: I Am Country's Mom," *World Magazine*, August 9, 1997.

Chapter 2: Character, Courage, and Conscience

1. Kenneth McFarland, *Eloquence in Public Speaking* (Englewood Cliffs, N.J.: Prentice-Hall, 1961), p. 49.

2. Michael Josephson, at www.josephsoninstitute.org.

3. Dr. Laura, interviewed by Craig Hamilton, *What Is Enlightenment Magazine*, Fall/Winter 1997.

4. The American Heritage Dictionary, see "conscience."

5. Dr. Laura Schlessinger, "article name?" *Take on the Day Newsletter*, Vol. 1, No. 2, January 1996, p. 3.

Chapter 3: Of Motherhood and God

1. Laura Schlessinger and Rabbi Stewart Vogel, *The Ten Commandments: The Significance of God's Laws in Everyday Life* (New York: HarperCollins, 1998), pp. xx—xxi.

2. C.S. Lewis, *The Weight of Glory* (Grand Rapids, Mich.: William B. Eerdmans Publishing Co., 1965), pp. 14-15.

Chapter 4: The Need for Objective Standards

1. C. R. Hembree, as quoted by Paul Lee Tan in *Encyclopedia of 7,700 Illustrations* (Garland, Tex.: Bible Communications, 1996).

2. Bill Watterson, *The Calvin and Hobbes Lazy Sunday Book* (Kansas City: Universal Press Syndicate, 1989), p. 110.

Chapter 5: "In My Never-to-Be-Humble Opinion"

1. Steven Waldman, Elise Ackerman, and Rita Rubin, "Abortion in America: So Many Women Have Them, So Few Talk about Them," *U.S. News and World Report,* January 19, 1998.

Chapter 6: Whirlwinds and Hurricanes

1. Pope John Paul II, quoted in *The Observer,* December 7, 1986.

2. Rose Macaulay, *The World My Wilderness,* 1950, Chapter 20 (as quoted in *The Columbia Dictionary of Quotations,* Copyright 1993 by Columbia University Press).

3. Robert L. Maginnis, *Insights,* Family Research Council, http://www.frc.org:80/insight/is96b1cr.html, February 6, 1996

Chapter 7: "I Am My Kid's Mom"

1. Kathleen Parker, *Debunking Yet Another Day-Care Study,* Sundy, March 7, 1999, Editorial Section, the *Orlando Sentinel.*

2. http://www.dncc96.org/cg96/accept/index.html

3. http://www.pub.whitehouse.gov/white-house-publications/1998/01

4. Walter Williams, "What's Happened To Us?", *Jewish World Review,* Nov. 24, 1998.

5. Meghan Cox Gurdon, "She's Back!" *The Women's Quarterly,* spring 1998, p. 7.

Chapter 8: Dr. Laura and the Christian Community

1. Gordon Fee and Douglas Stuart, *How to Read the Bible for All Its Worth* (Grand Rapids, M.I.: Zondervan, 1982), p. 19.